Berlitz®

Edinburgh

Front cover: Princes Stre

Below: The National Gall

D1440173

7400069411?X

The Scottish Parliament. One of Europe's most stunning and controversial modern buildings. See page 54.

The Scott Monument. A Gothic masterpiece. See page 65.

St Giles Cathedral. Featuring beautiful stained-glass windows and an ornate 20th-century chapel. See page 42.

Arthur's Seat. Climb this rock for a fantastic view of the city. See page 53.

Edinburgh Castle. Home of the Honours of Scotland and the One O'Clock Gun, and the site of the Military Tattoo. See page 30.

Charlotte Square. Located in Edinburgh's Georgian New Town, it is the finest square in the city. See page 68.

Festivals. Visitors flock to the city every summer for six major festivals. See page 85.

The Scottish National Gallery. One of the best art collections in Europe. See page 74.

The National Museum of Scotland. Telling the history of Scotland. See page 58.

The Palace of Holyroodhouse. The Queen's home in Scotland has ornate interiors and a long history. See page 48.

A PERFECT DAY

8.30am Breakfast

The ideal place to start a day of culture is at the Scottish Café inside the Scottish National Gallery, on Princes Street. Set yourself up with a traditional breakfast before a look around the gallery.

11.30am Castle Hill

Walk back down Castle Hill, passing attractions such as the Scotch Whisky Experience, Camera Obscura and Gladstone's Land, along the way. Take time to explore the vennels and wynds as you go.

12.30pm Shopping

Off George V Bridge, visit Victoria Street with its specialist shops, and continue on into the Grassmarket for lots of lunch options. Retrace your steps and continue to High Street, where St Giles Cathedral dominates.

10.00am Edinburgh Castle

Follow the Mound, crossing Princes Street Gardens towards the Old Town and climb the steep steps up to the castle. It's worth getting to the castle early to avoid the crowds. From here there are great views across the New Town below.

IN EDINBURGH

3.00pm Holyroodhouse

It is worth taking time to see the fine collection of royal artefacts (if the royal family are not in residence); alternatively, if weather allows, explore the huge expanse of Holyrood Park behind.

2.00pm Royal Mile

Continue down the Royal Mile, where you will find notable attractions including the Museum of Childhood, John Knox House, the Museum of Edinburgh and Canongate Tolbooth. Near the end of the road, the Scottish Parliament Building looms into view and at the foot of the Royal Mile stands the Palace of Holyroodhouse.

4.00pm Afternoon tea

Walk back up the Royal Mile. Just past the Scottish Parliament building is Clarinda's Tearoom, a great pit stop to indulge in tea and home-baked treats.

7.30pm Dinner

After freshening up at your hotel, head to the New Town – in and around George Street, good places to eat are endless. If Italian cooking is your preference, try the ever-popular Gusto or Contini. For a special occasion, Number One boasts a Michelin star.

9.30pm On the town

You couldn't be in a better spot to finish the night in a chic bar or nightclub. On George Street, pop into the Opal Lounge for cocktails and then move onto Lulu, a trendy club located beneath the Tigerlily hotel; or perhaps sip a Foxtrot Fizz or a Red Rum at Bramble in nearby Queen Street.

CONTENTS

Features

INTRODUCTION

Commenting on the city of his birth, Robert Louis Stevenson once declared himself baffled that 'this profusion of eccentricities, this dream in masonry and living rock is not a drop-scene in a theatre, but a city in the world of everyday reality'. There is something fantastical about the setting of Scotland's capital city. Hemmed in by the Pentland Hills to the south and the waters of the Firth of Forth to the north, Edinburgh is an extraordinary urban centre encompassing chunks of wilderness, ramshackle medieval tenements, stately Georgian townhouses and a castle-topped ridge. Yet, one of the delights of the city is that it is not simply a collection of heartless historic facades. It is instead a living, thriving community. The day-to-day lives of around half a million inhabitants are set against a rich backdrop of monuments, myths, martyrs and memories – those things which make Edinburgh such a magnet for visitors.

A Tale of Two Cities

Edinburgh, like Rome, is built on seven hills, an area welded together by volcanic activity 350 million years ago. Rising 435ft (133 metres) above sea level is the Castle Rock, used for thousands of years as a vantage point for defensive strongholds.

The town became the 'principal burgh' of the kingdom during the reign of James III (1460–88), and in the following years it blossomed. Complete districts from that time are still in place, brimming with churches, taverns, toll-houses and tenements, or 'lands'. These tall buildings were crammed with family upon family, with the gentry and merchant classes below and the commoners above. They are criss-crossed with numerous narrow alleys, or 'wynds', which are separated by open

Shops and tenements on Victoria Street

spaces where markets were held, royal decrees announced and criminals hanged in front of large, baying crowds.

Some 300 years later, towards the close of the 18th century, this medieval city witnessed the birth of a sibling. The 'New Town', which was planned by architect James Craig and embellished by Robert Adam, became one of the most elegant Georgian cities in the world, still very much complete today.

The New Town was the architectural embodiment of the Scottish Enlightenment, a profusion of intellectual talent and scholarly achievement. Although Edinburgh ceased to be the political capital in 1707 (following the Act of Union, which saw Scotland united with England under one monarch and parliament in London), the city instead became a crucible of thought, home to pioneering philosophers, scientists, architects, engineers, painters and authors.

While the rich abandoned the ramshackle Old Town to the poor, flitting to the neoclassical grandeur of the New Town, the 19th century also saw a city-wide boom in the middle classes, working in banking, insurance and law. Inspired by the economic doctrines of Adam Smith, lawyers and accountants made a fortune investing the wealth of Scottish industrialists in foreign ventures. Edinburgh continues to house one of the largest financial communities in Europe.

Auld Reekie

In old Edinburgh almost every room in every dwelling was kept warm with an open fire, and thousands of sooty plumes rose daily above the city. Following the Industrial Revolution, factories and smoke-belching trains added to the problem. As a result, Edinburgh was given the nickname 'Auld Reekie' (Old Smoky). But after World War II the city introduced a clean-air policy and removed the sooty residue from stone buildings in the New Town, consigning Edinburgh's dark and dirty reputation to the past.

National Treasure

During the summer months Edinburgh's population trebles as tourists flood into the city to see the many national treasures contained within its boundaries. A large proportion will visit Edinburgh Castle, Scotland's most popular attraction and home to the Honours of Scotland (crown jewels) and the Stone of Destiny, the symbolic coronation seat returned to Scotland in 1996 after 700 years of English possession.

The Military Tattoo on the Castle Esplanade

Edinburgh has three national art galleries – the Scottish National Gallery, the Scottish National Portrait Gallery and the Scottish National Gallery of Modern Art, comprising Modern One and Modern Two – which feature the work of masters ranging from Titian to Dali. You'll also find the Royal Palace of Holyroodhouse, one of the British royal family's most ancient residences, and nearby the new home to the Scottish Parliament. Edinburgh's major museums include the National Museum of Scotland, which documents the country's history from earliest times to the present day.

Festival City

The people of Edinburgh have often been characterised by their fellow countrymen as reserved, prim and haughty. One reason for this could be that they have traditionally pursued such conservative, respectable vocations as banking, medicine, law and academia. But their wealth of earnest achievement doesn't mean that the people of Edinburgh lack verve or the ability to enjoy themselves. It is simply that the serious aspects of life are given

A street artist entertains visitors

their proper due before the fun can begin. Edinburgh's inhabitants are very welcoming to visitors and tend to be quite genuine and unaffected. The city's urbane residents enjoy their galleries, theatres and exhibitions as much as visitors do. Their restaurants feature internationally renowned chefs who create dishes using some of the finest fish and meat in the world, ranging from wild salmon to Aberdeen Angus beef and Highland game and venison. People here love to socialise, getting together in the hundreds of characterful pubs, bars and cafés.

Established by Sir Rudolph Bing in the wake of World War II, Edinburgh's annual arts festival aimed to attract major names in music, drama and dance. By 1987, the Edinburgh International Festival had grown into the largest annual arts event in the world with hundreds of performances in numerous venues across the city during August.

Today, the main arts festival is only part of a veritable circus of summer activities. Regiments of soldiers in full dress regalia march to the sound of pipe and drum in the Military Tattoo, and film connoisseurs gather for a key event in the international movie calendar. The Mela Festival is an infectious delight of world music and international dance held on Leith Links. However, the Festival Fringe is by far the most visible and most attended of Edinburgh's August Festivals. It encompasses thousands of performances ranging from the avant-garde to the downright irreverent. And each year at festival time, Edinburgh gives its streets over to stilt walkers, satirists, bagpipers and barbershop quartets, along with a vast influx of visitors – belying its reputation for being sober and staid.

Another great time to visit Edinburgh is at the turn of the year, when the city hosts one of the world's biggest New Year's Eve parties, Hogmanay. The whole population comes out into the streets to celebrate what the locals call Hogmanay, with a huge display of fireworks illuminating the city's historic skyline.

Edinburgh is a city of contrast, on the one hand a historic Unesco World Heritage Site and on the other a lively modern city with a festival heart. With a renewed vigour that is attracting strong investment, there are exciting times ahead for the city. This began with the introduction of the tram system and the Cowgate development, rising from the ashes of the 2002 fire. Ongoing projects include the St James city centre regeneration due for completion in 2020. Princes Street continues to be revamped and the go-ahead has been given for the controversial Caltongate complex. Edinburgh is energised and vies with London and Paris as a top European holiday destination.

Performers at the Fringe

A BRIEF HISTORY

The city of Edinburgh grew up around the steep, ragged cliff of the Castle Rock and its easily defended summit. Archaeological excavations have revealed evidence of habitation here as long ago as 900 BC. Very little, however, is known about the Rock and its inhabitants in the centuries between its first occupation and the time of the MacAlpin kings. A few shadowy details have been left to us by the Romans and by an epic poem from the seventh century.

Romans and Britons

In AD 78–84 the Romans invaded Scotland where they met a group called the Picts, whom they drove north. They consolidated their gains by building the Antonine Wall across the waist of Scotland between the Firth of Forth and the River Clyde in about AD 150. Roman legions encountered the strongholds of the Castle Rock and Arthur's Seat, held by a tribe of ancient Britons – the Votadini. Little is known of them, but they were probably the ancestors of the Gododdin, whose feats are told in a 7th-century Old Welsh manuscript. Their capital, Din Eidyn, fell to the Angles in 638 and became part of the Anglian kingdom of Northumbria. It was the first of many times that the site would change hands.

Din Eidyn

Din Eidyn (the 'Fort of Eidyn') – almost certainly the Castle Rock – was the Gododdin tribe's capital. The name lives on in the *Edin* of Edinburgh.

The MacAlpin Kings

Four distinct peoples once inhabited the land now known as Scotland: the Picts in the north, the Britons in the southwest, the invading Angles in the southeast, and the Scots in the west. The Scots were Gaelic-speaking immigrants from the north of Ireland. Kenneth Mac-Alpin, who ruled as King of Scots at Dunadd, acquired the Pictish throne in 843, uniting Scotland north of the River Forth into a single kingdom. He moved his capital – along with the Stone of Destiny (on which Scottish kings were crowned) – to the sacred Pict site of Scone, close to Perth. His great-great-great-grandson, Malcolm II (1005–34), defeated the Angles at the Battle of Carham in 1018 and extended Scottish territory as far south as the River Tweed. These new lands included the stronghold of Edinburgh.

Robert the Bruce

Malcolm II's grandson, Malcolm Canmore (1058–93), often visited Edinburgh with his wife Margaret, a Saxon princess. They crossed the Forth from Dunfermline at the narrows known to this day as Queensferry. Margaret was a deeply pious woman who was subsequently canonised, and her youngest son, David I (1124–53), founded a church in her name on the highest point of the Castle Rock (St Margaret's Chapel). David also founded the Abbey of Holyrood and created several royal burghs (towns with special trading privileges), including Edinburgh and Canongate; the latter was under the jurisdiction of the monks, or 'canons', of Holyrood.

The Castle in ruins

When in power, Robert the Bruce was so concerned by the ease with which the English could advance on Edinburgh and dominate the country from the Castle that he demolished it, except for the small chapel of St Margaret.

At this point in time, Edinburgh was still a modest town, but David's successor, Malcolm IV (1153–65), made its castle his main residence. By the end of the 12th century, Edinburgh's castle was used as a royal treasury. The town's High Street stretched from the castle along the ridge to the east (today the Royal Mile), past the parish church of St Giles, and out to the Netherbow, where Edinburgh ended and Canongate began.

Wars of Independence

In 1286 the MacAlpin dynasty ended, leaving Scotland without a ruler. There were a number of claimants to the throne, among them John Balliol, Lord of Galloway, and Robert de Brus, Lord of Annandale. The guardians of Scotland were unable to decide who should succeed and asked the English king, Edward I, to adjudicate. Edward, seeing this invitation as a chance to assert his claim as overlord of Scotland, chose John Balliol, whom he judged to be the weaker of the two.

Edward treated King John as a vassal. However, when Edward went to war with France in 1294 and summoned John along with other knights, the Scottish king decided he had had enough. He ignored Edward's summons and instead negotiated a treaty with the French king, the beginning of a long association between France and Scotland that would become known as the 'Auld Alliance'.

Edward was furious and his reprisal was swift and bloody. In 1296 he led a force of nearly 30,000 men into Scotland and captured the castles of Roxburgh, Edinburgh and Stirling. The Stone of Destiny and the Scottish crown jewels were stolen, and Scotland's Great Seal was broken up. Oaths of fealty were demanded from Scottish nobles, while English officials were installed to oversee the running of the country. Scotland became little more than an English county.

But the Scots did not take this insult lying down. Bands of rebels (such as those led by William Wallace) began to attack the English garrisons and make raids into English territory. When Wallace was captured, the Scots looked for a new leader and discovered one in Robert the Bruce, grandson of the Robert de Brus rejected by Edward in 1292. He was crowned King of Scots at Scone in 1306 and began his campaign to drive the English out of Scotland.

Edward I died in 1307 and was succeeded by his son, Edward II, who in 1314 led an army of 25,000 men to confront Bruce's army at Bannockburn, near Stirling. Though outnumbered, the Scots sent the English packing. Robert the Bruce continued to harass the English until they were forced to sue for peace. A truce was declared, and the Treaty of Northampton was negotiated at Edinburgh in 1328.

Although many Scottish nobles were dedicated to the cause of independence, others either bore grudges against the ruling king or held lands in England that they feared to lose. These

A 15th-century illumination of St Margaret

divisions – later hardened by religious schism – would forever deny Scotland a truly united voice.

When Robert the Bruce died in 1329, his son and heir, David II, was only five years old. Within a few years the wars with England resumed, aggravated by civil war at home as Edward Balliol (son of John) tried to take the Scottish throne with the help of the English king, Edward III.

The Stewart Dynasty

During these stormy years, the castle of Edinburgh was occupied several times by English garrisons. In 1341 it was taken from the English by William of Douglas. The young David II returned from exile in France and made it his principal royal residence, building a tower house (David's Tower) on the site of what is now the Half Moon Battery. He died in 1371 and was succeeded by his nephew, Robert II. David's sister Marjory had married Walter the Steward, and their son was the first of the long line of Stewart (later spelt *Stuart*) monarchs who would reign over Scotland – and, subsequently, Great Britain – until the 'Glorious Revolution' of 1688.

The strength and wealth of Scotland increased during the reigns of the first Stewart kings. Castles were built and weapons acquired, including the gun, 'Mons Meg'. Edinburgh emerged as Scotland's main political centre and was declared by James III (1460–88) to be 'the principal burgh of our kingdom'.

James IV (1488–1513) confirmed Edinburgh's status as the capital of Scotland by constructing a royal palace at Holyrood. He cemented a peace treaty with England by marrying Margaret Tudor, daughter of Henry VII – the so-called Marriage of the Thistle and the Rose – but this did not prevent him from making a raid into England in 1513. The attack culminated in the Battle of Flodden, near the River Tweed, where the king was killed. Fearing invasion, the Edinburgh town council built a wall (the 'Flodden Wall') around the city boundaries.

Mons Meg – a gift to James IV from the Duke of Burgundy

Yet again a child – the infant James V – succeeded to the throne, and Scottish nobles were divided as to whether Scotland should draw closer to England or seek help from her old ally, France. The adult James leant towards France and in 1537 took a French wife, Mary of Guise. She bore two sons who both died in infancy, but by the time she was about to give birth to their third child, her husband lay dying at Falkland Palace. On 8 December 1542 a messenger arrived with news that the queen had produced a daughter at the palace of Linlithgow. A few days later the king was dead, leaving a week-old baby girl to inherit the Scottish crown.

Mary, Queen of Scots

At the age of nine months, the baby Mary Stuart was crowned Queen of Scots at the Chapel Royal, Stirling. When the news reached London, Henry VIII saw his chance to subdue Scotland again and negotiated a marriage between the infant

MARY QUEEN OF SCOTS

Mary, Queen of Scots, depicted on the Great Tapestry of Scotland

Mary and his son Edward. The Scots refused, and Henry sent an army rampaging through Scotland on a campaign known as the 'Rough Wooing'. The English king ordered his general to 'burn Edinburgh town so there may remain forever a perpetual memory of the vengeance of God lightened upon the Scots'.

But more was at stake than simply Scotland's independence: there was now a religious schism within Britain. In order to divorce Catherine of Aragon and marry Anne Boleyn, Henry VIII had broken with Rome and brought the English church under his own control. England was thus now a Protestant country, caught between Catholic France and the Scots with their new Catholic queen.

The Scots themselves were divided, many embracing Protestantism while others remained staunchly Catholic. However, fear of the rampaging English army led the Scots again to seek help from their old allies in France, and the young queen married the Dauphin François, son of the French king.

François II became king of France in 1559 but died soon after. In 1561 the 18-year-old Mary returned to a Scotland in the grip of the Reformation, as Protestant leaders had taken control of the Scottish Parliament and abolished the authority of the pope. Her Protestant cousin, Elizabeth Tudor, was on the English throne, but Elizabeth – the 'Virgin Queen' – had no heir. Mary was next in line for the English crown, and Elizabeth suspected her intentions.

The six years of Mary's reign were turbulent ones. She clashed early on with Edinburgh's Protestant reformer, John Knox, who held sway in St Giles, but later adopted an uneasy policy of religious tolerance. In 1565 she married her young cousin Henry, Lord Darnley, much to the chagrin of Elizabeth (Darnley was a grandson of Margaret Tudor and thus also had a claim to the English throne). On 19 June 1566, in Edinburgh Castle, Mary gave birth to a son, Prince James.

Within a year, however, Darnley was murdered. Mary immediately immersed herself in controversy by marrying the Earl of Bothwell, the chief suspect. Mary was forced to abdicate in 1567, and the infant prince was crowned as James VI.

Mary sought asylum in England, only to be imprisoned by Elizabeth. The English queen kept her cousin in captivity for 20 years and finally had her beheaded on a trumped-up charge of treason. So it was bitterly ironic when Elizabeth died without an heir and James, Mary's Catholic son, inherited the English throne.

In 1603 James VI of Scotland was thus crowned James I of England, marking the Union of the Crowns. Although Scotland was still a separate kingdom, the two countries would from that day be ruled by the same monarch.

The Covenanters

The population of Edinburgh grew fast between 1500 and 1650, and a maze of tall, unsanitary tenements

Child monarchs

A recurring feature of Scottish history is the inheritance of the throne by a child. Mary Stuart was just six days old when she succeeded James V.

James VI of Scotland who became James I of England

sprouted along the spine of the High Street. The castle was extended, and in 1582 the Town's College (the precursor of the University of Edinburgh) was founded. James died in 1625, and was succeeded by his son, Charles I, who proved an incompetent ruler. In 1637 his attempt to force the Scottish Presbyterian Church into accepting an English liturgy and the rule of bishops led to civil revolt and rioting.

The next year, a large group of Scottish churchmen and nobles signed the National Covenant, pledging allegiance to the Presbyterian faith. At first, the so-called Covenanters sided with Oliver Cromwell's Parliamentarians in the civil war that had erupted across the border. But when the English revolutionaries beheaded Charles I in 1649, the Scots rallied round his son, Charles II. Cromwell's forces invaded Scotland, crushed the Covenanters and went on to take Edinburgh. Scotland suffered 10 years of military rule under Cromwell's Commonwealth.

Scotland's troubles continued after Charles II's restoration to the throne in 1660. The Covenanters faced severe persecution at the hands of the king's supporters, who had decided to follow his father's policy of imposing bishops on the Scots. Hundreds of Covenanters were imprisoned and executed.

In the end England underwent the 'Glorious Revolution' of 1688, when Catholic James II (Scotland's James VII) was deposed and the Protestant William of Orange (1689–1702) took the British crown. Presbyterianism was established as Scotland's official state church and the Covenanters prevailed.

Act of Union

On 1 May 1707 England and Scotland were formally joined together by the 'Act of Union' – establishing the Union of Parliaments – and the United Kingdom was born. Although Scotland retained its own legal system, education system and national Presbyterian Church, the move was opposed by the majority of Scots. The supporters of the deposed James VII and his successors, exiled in France, were known as the 'Jacobites'. Several times during the next 40 years they tried to restore the Stuart dynasty to the British throne, though by this time the crown had passed to the German House of Hanover. James Edward Stuart, known as the 'Old Pretender', travelled up the Firth of Forth in 1708 but was driven back by British ships and bad weather. Another campaign was held in 1715 under the Jacobite Earl of Mar, but it was the 1745 rising of Prince Charles Edward Stuart, the 'Young Pretender', which became the stuff of legend.

The prince, known as Bonnie Prince Charlie the grandson of James VII), raised an army of Jacobite Highlanders and swept through

The History of the Church of Scotland at John Knox House

Scotland. They occupied Edinburgh (but not the castle) and defeated a government army at the Battle of Prestonpans. In November of that year he invaded England, capturing Carlisle and driving south as far as Derby, only 125 miles (200km) short of London.

Finding his forces outnumbered and overextended here, the young prince beat a tactical retreat, but the English army hounded him relentlessly. The final showdown – at Culloden in 1746 – saw the Jacobite army slaughtered. Prince Charlie fled and was pursued over the Highlands before escaping in a French ship. He died in Rome in 1788, disillusioned and drunk.

Scottish Enlightenment

The Jacobite uprisings found little support in such Lowland cities as Edinburgh. Here there was a growing sense that the Union was around to stay. Within 10 years of the Young

Burke and Hare

In the early 19th century, Edinburgh was at the forefront of the medical world, making great strides in the understanding of diseases and infections. As part of this research process, the medical establishment needed cadavers for dissection, and a grisly black market developed, headed by William Burke and William Hare.

At first they earned their money by digging up freshly buried corpses to sell to physicians, but when demand outstripped supply, they began to roam the streets around the Grassmarket looking for suitable victims, whom they lured into dark alleyways and strangled.

Only when Hare testified in court against his partner was the unsavoury business brought to the public eye. Genteel society was outraged. Hare got away with his nefarious deeds, but Burke was hanged in the Grassmarket in 1829 and his body used for medical research.

Pretender's occupation of Holyrood, the town council of Edinburgh proposed a plan to relieve the chronic overcrowding of the Royal Mile tenements by constructing a New Town on land north of the castle. In 1767 a design by a young architect, James Craig, was approved and work began.

Robert Burns

This architectural renaissance in Edinburgh was followed by an intellectual flowering in the sciences, philosophy and medicine that revolutionised Western society in the late 18th century. Famous Edinburgh residents of this period – later known as the Scottish Enlightenment – included David Hume, eminent British philosopher and author of *A Treatise of Human Nature*, pioneering economist Adam Smith, author of *The Wealth of Nations*, and scientist Joseph Black, who discovered the concept of latent heat. Robert Burns' poems and Walter Scott's novels rekindled interest in Scotland's history and nationhood.

The Modern City

In the 19th century Edinburgh was swept up in the Industrial Revolution. The coalfields of Lothian and Fife fuelled the growth of baking, distilling, printing and machine-making industries. Smoke from factories gave rise to Edinburgh's nickname 'Auld Reekie'. With the arrival of the railways in the mid-1800s, the city grew as new lines led to the spread of suburbs.

During the 20th century Edinburgh built and consolidated its position as a European centre of finance, learning and culture. The rise of the Edinburgh International Festival and the extraordinary growth of the Fringe around it, set against a rich backdrop of architecture and history, established the city as one of the top tourist destinations in the UK.

Edinburgh never ceased to think of itself defiantly as the nation's capital and the latter part of the 20th century saw a concerted (though peaceful) effort to gain self-determination for Scotland. In 1979 the nationalists were in disarray when a referendum was defeated. Further efforts came to nought during the following years of Conservative rule at Westminster, although the Stone of Destiny was returned to Scottish soil in 1996 – 700 years after it had been taken south by the English.

The election of New Labour in 1997 was a turning point. The new government organised a referendum on Scottish devolution and a majority voted for the creation of a Scottish Parliament. Political power returned to Edinburgh after nearly 300 years. The new Parliament opened July 1999 and in October 2004 it moved to a state-of-the-art building at Holyrood. Passions ran high in the build up to the September 2014 referendum for Scottish independence. With a high turnout of 84.5 percent Scotland voted to stay in the Union with England with 55 percent for the 'no to Scottish independence' campaign and 45 percent for the 'yes'. Devolution from England, however, is expected to be further extended.

Traditions live on

Historical Landmarks

900 BC Late-Bronze/early-Iron Age settlement on Castle Rock.

1st–2nd centuries AD Roman occupation of southern Scotland; hill fort of the Votadini tribe on Castle Rock.

843 Scotland north of the Forth united under Kenneth MacAlpin.

1124–53 Reign of David I, founder of Abbey of Holyrood.

1297 Scots rebels under Wallace defeat English at Stirling Bridge.

1314 Scots victory under Robert the Bruce at Bannockburn.

1513 Scots suffer defeat at Flodden; Edinburgh builds city walls.

1544 The Rough Wooing: Henry VIII's forces sack Edinburgh.

1559–72 John Knox is minister of St Giles.

1560 Protestantism is established as Scotland's national faith.

1561–7 Mary, Queen of Scots, lives in Holyrood Palace.

1603 Union of the Crowns: James VI of Scotland becomes James I of England.

1638 The National Covenant is signed at Greyfriars Kirkyard.

1689 William of Orange invited to take over government of Scotland; civil war between William and Jacobites.

1707 'Act of Union' and creation of the UK; Scottish Parliament dissolved.

1745 Jacobite uprising; Bonnie Prince Charlie's army occupies Holyrood.

1767 Construction of Edinburgh's New Town begins.

1844 Sir Walter Scott monument is completed.

1890 Forth Bridge opens.

1947 The first Edinburgh International Festival.

1995 Edinburgh's Old and New Towns become a Unesco World Heritage site.

1997 Referendum on Scottish devolution receives a majority vote.

1999 Scottish elections held; first 'new' Parliament opens 1 July.

2002 Fire devastates the Cowgate area of the city.

2004 Opening of the iconic Parliament Building.

2008 The pro-independence Scottish National Party (SNP) becomes the largest party in the Scottish Parliament.

2014 A new network of trams becomes fully operational; Edinburgh votes to stay in the Union in a national referendum.

WHERE TO GO

Edinburgh is a city of several distinct historical districts that are all eminently walkable. You can divide your visit into three or four separate tours, each of which could fill either an afternoon or an entire day. There are also bus tours around the city to help you get your bearings before you visit the attractions. Tour buses stand in line on Waverley Street opposite the main railway station (see page 124).

THE OLD TOWN

Although no one can be certain how old the settlement of Edinburgh actually is, it is possible that people have been living there for over 5,000 years. Even before that, the site of Edinburgh's **Old Town** has its own fascinating story to tell in terms of its geological origin. The Castle Rock and Arthur's Seat are the remains of lava streams that hardened after the two volcanoes around them became dormant and cold. During the last Ice Age, huge glaciers covered the region, moving west to east across the land and gouging trenches on either side of the volcanic mounds. They resisted the great power of the ice and caused a long stream of sediment to collect. At the end of the Ice Age (some 13,000 years ago), the glaciers melted, leaving a long ridge of sediment sloping gradually from the top of the volcanic hills.

The original city of Edinburgh grew from the tiny community that first clung to the ridge, reaching down in a ribbon of development towards the Abbey of Holyrood, at the foot of the hill in the east. In the 16th century, the Flodden Wall – now almost completely destroyed – protected the population. Combined with the geological setting of the city, the wall

The Canongate Tolbooth

stifled development. Instead of expanding outwards, the city had no choice but to grow upwards.

And so, Edinburgh's famous tenements (or 'lands') began to be built. At least six storeys high, they were reached through narrow alleys called 'closes' or 'wynds' that became the focus of city life. A constant cycle of building, decay, collapse and rebuilding – plus the occasional catastrophic fire – gave the Old Town its characteristic irregular layout and chimney-strewn skyline.

Edinburgh Castle

With steep, defendable sides and strategic vantage points, the site of Edinburgh Castle was contested for hundreds of years by generations of Picts, Scots, Britons and Angles. Dominating the skyline, the dramatically rising cliff of black basalt stone made the castle impregnable to all but the most wily commander. It was the seat of power for anyone who ruled the region,

The Gate House of Edinburgh Castle

although it was not until the 11th century that Edinburgh settled down to become the capital of an independent Scotland, with a royal residence constructed within the castle walls.

After the 'Act of Union' with England in 1707, the castle lost its strategic importance. Much of the present-day complex dates from the 18th and 19th centuries when the royal castle was

Mons Meg

A gun weighing 6.6 tons (6,040kg), Mons Meg was a gift to James II in 1457 from his wife's uncle, Philip the Good, Duke of Burgundy. Manufactured in Mons (now in Belgium), the gun was state-of-the-art for the time, but weighed so much that it could be transported only 3 miles (5km) per day; often the fighting had ended before it could be brought into play.

transformed into a garrison fortress with barracks and modern defences. The Victorians, who had a penchant for reworking the history and legends of Scotland, also added romantic, neo-Gothic touches.

Today **Edinburgh Castle** ❶ (www.edinburghcastle.gov.uk; daily Apr–Sept 9.30am–6pm; Oct–Mar 9.30am–5pm) is one of the most popular attractions in Scotland. A visit to the castle will take at least two hours, and most people take advantage of the audio guide (for a small extra fee).

Your first view of the castle will be the **Gate House**, which you pass through to reach the inner wards. Built between 1886 and 1888, the structure was a Victorian attempt to recapture the medieval castle style, although it was more decorative than defensive. The dry ditches in front, however, date from the 1650s. In the 1920s bronze statues of two Scottish heroes – William Wallace and Robert the Bruce – were added to the facade.

Once inside, you will find yourself in the lower ward, the area of the castle that has been most heavily bombarded in many military campaigns. The Old Guard House houses one of three gift shops in the castle grounds. The walkway

Firing of the One O'Clock Gun

here once had a ditch and drawbridge to protect the inner gate, called **Portcullis Gate**, which was reconstructed in the late 16th century on 14th-century foundations. It was the main entrance to the castle and a formidable obstacle to the enemy.

Passing through Portcullis Gate, you enter the middle ward of the castle. Ahead to your right is the **Argyll Battery**, with a line of muzzle-loading 18-lb guns pointing out northwards over the skyline of the New Town (a prime spot for spectacular photos). To your left are the Lang Stairs, which lead up to the medieval castle. Walk along past the battery to the Cart Shed, built in the aftermath of the Jacobite uprising in 1746. It now houses a café but was originally used to store the provisions carts. Beside the café is Mills Mount Battery, the location of the **One O'Clock Gun**, fired daily except Sunday, Good Friday and Christmas Day. Be prepared, for it is indeed noisy.

The cobbled street winds steeply upwards, past the Governor's House and the New Barracks, where you will find the **National War Museum** and the **Regimental Museum of the Royal Scots Dragoon Guards**. Eventually you will reach **Foog's Gate** – the name and age of the gate remain a source of debate – to enter the upper ward and the oldest parts of the castle. To the left is a gift shop, and directly ahead is tiny **St Margaret's Chapel**, said to have been built by David I in the early 12th century in honour of his mother, Queen Margaret, who died in 1093. It is the oldest building in Edinburgh and is still the site of weddings and baptisms. Although the chapel has been renovated since its construction, you will find a wonderful example of a Romanesque arch in the interior. The stained-glass windows, one featuring a likeness of Margaret, were inserted into the existing openings in the 1920s. Just outside the entrance is the Mons Meg gun.

In an open area south of the chapel is the **Half-Moon Battery**, built on the site of David's Tower, which was once the largest and most formidable structure in the castle. Begun in 1368, it was the main royal lodging for centuries until it was left a wreck during the 'Lang Siege' of 1571–3.

Crown Square

At the very pinnacle of the upper ward is **Crown Square**, a beautiful collection of buildings housing the treasures of Scotland. On your right as you enter the square is the **Scottish National War Memorial**, the highest building in the city. The building was originally a barracks but was suitably refurbished by

St Margaret, mother of David I

Armour in the Great Hall

Sir Robert Lorimer in 1923 to commemorate the Scots who fell in World War I; the halls of remembrance also commemorate those who died in World War II and all other conflicts. Inside, there are leather-bound regimental books with each serviceperson's name duly inscribed. Splendidly ornate stone friezes depict battle scenes of World War I, with each branch of the forces represented.

Opposite the memorial is the **Great Hall**, built in 1503 for the wedding reception of James IV and the English Margaret Tudor. It was later used as the ceremonial and legislative chamber. The original 'hammer-beam' wooden roof is the highlight of the design, with thick beams and painted decorations. Note the monogram of James – IR4 – on some of the stone brackets, along with the red rose and the thistle signifying the new alliance of Scotland and England. The hall was used as a barracks through much of its later history before being renovated in 1887. The interior decor says much more about the Victorians' romantic image of Scotland than it does about how the room would have really looked.

On the west side of the square is the **Queen Anne Building**, with a café for lunch or afternoon tea. Also here is the entrance to the **Prison of War Exhibition** in the Castle Vaults, which explores the experiences of sailors of various nationalities who were incarcerated in the castle, having been captured during the Seven Years War (1756–63), the American War of Independence (1776–83) and the Napoleonic Wars

(1793–1815). The POWs' living quarters are recreated, with cramped cots and hammocks, and there are original prison doors graffitied by the prisoners.

Along the east side of Crown Square is the **Royal Palace**, home to the crown jewels of Scotland. The palace, much altered over the generations, was generally used as a residence only at times of dynastic importance or danger, when Holyrood, down in the lowland, was difficult to defend. On 19 June 1566 Mary Stuart gave birth to her son James (the future James VI of Scotland and James I of England) in the small antechamber off a larger room known as **Queen Mary's Room**. The last monarch to stay in the palace was Charles I, in 1633.

On the upper floors (once the royal chambers) there is an exhibition telling the story of the **Honours of Scotland**. These crown jewels are said to be the oldest complete set – crown, sceptre and sword – in Europe, unchanged since 1640. They lie on blue velvet in a secure glass cabinet in the Crown Room. The Scottish crown was fashioned of gold mined in Scotland, greatly embellished during the reign of

Edinburgh Military Tattoo

In 1950 the city established a Military Tattoo at the same time as the Festival, and the two have now become an inseparable combination. The tattoo is a highly polished show of military marching, pageantry, mock battles and horsemanship, accompanied by the sounds of pipe-and-drum bands from around the world. All this happens nightly (except Sunday) against the backdrop of the magnificently floodlit castle in an arena erected in the Esplanade. Tickets (which sell out months in advance) can be bought from the ticket office at 33–34 Market Street, behind Waverley Station (tel: 0131 225 1188; www.edintattoo.co.uk). The Tattoo visitor centre is housed in the same building and traces the event's history; it also has a gift shop.

Scotland's James III (1460–88). The sceptre and sword were each papal gifts – the former in 1494 and the latter in 1507; these reinforced the links between Scotland and Rome. Following union with England in 1707, however, there was little use for the Scottish regalia. They were locked in a trunk in a sealed room in Edinburgh Castle for 111 years before Sir Walter Scott received permission to open the room in 1818.

Next to the regalia sits the **Stone of Destiny**, or Stone of Scone, which historically served as the seat on which Scottish kings were crowned, a symbol of the land over which they would rule. In 1296 the stone was captured by the English from its resting place in Scone Abbey and taken to London. It has been used during crowning ceremonies for all English (then British) monarchs since that time, sitting under the coronation throne throughout the ceremony. In 1996 the stone was returned to Scotland amid great pomp, though it will make the journey to London's Westminster Abbey when the next coronation of a British monarch takes place.

On the lower floor of the Royal Palace, **Laich Hall** has been restored as closely as possible to its 1617 decor, using traditional techniques and colours. This was where the monarch met advisers and diplomats.

Leaving the castle, you will walk across the **Esplanade**, a broad open area originally created for regimental drill practice. Today, it is usually used as a car park, but it offers superb views of both Princes Street to the north and the Old Town to the south. In summer the Esplanade is filled by a temporary arena erected for performances of the Military Tattoo and occasional pop concerts.

The Royal Mile

The town of Edinburgh eventually spread out below the castle, with a main street leading out the entrance and down to the Palace of Holyroodhouse. In the 16th century this thoroughfare became known as the **Royal Mile** because it was the route used by royalty to make their way from the castle to Holyrood. A mile long, the city's oldest thoroughfare comprises four sections: Castlehill, Lawnmarket, the High Street and the Canongate. In former times it even crossed the old outer boundary of Edinburgh before it reached the palace.

Since the route has never seen major redevelopment, it has grown haphazardly but organically over the centuries. Some buildings date from the 16th century, but it is also lined with buildings of almost every era, including numerous 17th- and 18th-century tenements sometimes 13 storeys high. These were the residential areas of the city, considered

Deacon Brodie's Tavern

desirable when first built. Later, they were often home to many large families, rife with overcrowding and unsanitary conditions.

Before you leave the castle's Esplanade, look out for the small bronze fountain on the wall to the left of the entrance. This is the **Witches Well**, which marks the spot where, between 1479 and 1722, women condemned for practising black magic were burned at the stake.

Beyond the Esplanade you enter the first section of the Royal Mile, narrow, cobbled **Castlehill**. On your left you will find the **Tartan Weaving Mill**, where you can follow the journey of wool from the sheep to the finished product. You can watch a tartan pattern being woven by machine and then choose from around 170 tartans in the shop. There are also gift shops selling quality Scottish products, such as Aran wool and silver jewellery. Built in 1850, the building itself was at one time the major water storage facility for the New Town.

Next to the weaving centre, across narrow Ramsay Lane, are the **Camera Obscura and World of Illusions** ❷ (www.camera-obscura.co.uk; daily Apr–Oct 9.30am–7pm, July and Aug 9am–9pm; Nov–Mar 10am–6pm) set high above the tenement chimney stacks. A series of lenses and prisms projects a live image of the city onto a concave viewing screen inside the camera. It was built in the 1850s, when cameras were the height of fashion. Several people at one time can sit

Advocate's Close, at the top of the High Street

inside and watch the city at work. The experience is best when the weather is bright. There is a viewing platform around the camera, allowing first-hand viewing of the cityscape, including close-ups of stonework not otherwise possible to view. Visit the Camera Obscura at noon when there are fewer shadows.

Across the road you'll find the **Scotch Whisky Experience** ❸ (www.scotchwhisky experience.co.uk; daily Sept–May 10am–6pm, June–Aug until 6.30pm), which tells the story of the development of Scottish whisky. The various tours naturally all include a chance to taste this

The Camera Obscura and World of Illusions

complex drink and end with a barrel ride that whisks you through 300 years of the 'water of life'. Visitors can also buy whisky – over 300 varieties are available.

At the bottom of Castlehill, where the road meets Johnston Terrace, is the old, soot-black Tolbooth Kirk (or church), which has the highest steeple in the city at 239ft (73 metres). In the late 1990s the church underwent a massive renovation and was re-christened **The Hub**, acting as the permanent centre and offices for the Edinburgh International Festival, with a booking office (Mon–Sat 10am–5pm, extended hours during festival; see page 132) and café, and as a venue for the Jazz and Blues Festival.

The Writers' Museum holds relics of three famed authors

Lawnmarket

Beyond the Hub, the Royal Mile is known as Lawnmarket. This was once the commercial centre of the Old Town, including a weekly fabric market. There are several old lands found down the narrow wynds leading off the main street. **Gladstone's Land ❹** (daily mid-Mar–Oct 10am–5pm, July–Aug until 6.30pm), once the home of a wealthy 17th-century merchant, still has a period shopfront, and inside it is authentically furnished to give an impression of life 300 years ago. It also includes a gift shop with an array of merchandise.

Behind Gladstone's Land is Lady Stair's Close, which leads to Lady Stair's House, home to the **Writers' Museum ❺** (www.edinburghmuseums.org.uk; Mon–Sat 10am–5pm, Sun during Aug noon–5pm; free). The beautifully renovated house (dating from 1622) contains manuscripts and personal effects from three of Scotland's best-known authors: Robert Burns, Sir Walter Scott and Robert Louis Stevenson. The Stevenson exhibition on the lower floor is particularly interesting, with photographs of the author travelling around the world before his untimely death at the age of 44 in Samoa. A room on the top floor holds temporary exhibitions about other writers and literary themes.

Next to the Writers' Museum is **James Court**. The philosopher David Hume lived here and was regularly visited by the economist Adam Smith and by Dr Samuel Johnson. The court must have been a hotbed of social reform at the time.

At the corner of Lawnmarket and Bank Street is **Deacon Brodie's Tavern**. Named after the city gentleman and infamous burglar, it is one of the best-known pubs in the city. Look left down Bank Street to see the ornate facade of the **Bank of Scotland** headquarters, a symbol of the city's continuing important position in the financial world. The bank was founded in 1695, and is the only body established by the old Scottish Parliament that still exists today. The founding Act is on display, among a wealth of banking paraphernalia, in the **Museum on the Mound** (www.museumonthemound.com; Tue–Fri 10am–5pm, Sat–Sun 1–5pm; free). For those who can't imagine what a million pounds looks like, one display cabinet contains the sum in (cancelled) banknotes.

A Split Personality

When Robert Louis Stevenson wrote *The Strange Case of Dr Jekyll and Mr Hyde* in 1886, it shocked genteel society. Little did people realise that although he set the book in London, he had based his story on the real-life case of an Edinburgh man.

Deacon William Brodie was a respectable cabinetmaker and locksmith who, when he closed his shop in the evening, lived another life. After dark he frequented the less respectable parts of town – gambling, cockfighting and fathering five illegitimate children. He funded this lifestyle by stealing from his respectable customers, taking copies of the keys of cabinets and strongboxes sold in his shop and creeping into their houses to relieve them of their valuables.

Deacon Brodie was caught in the act in 1788 and was hanged in front of a huge crowd. Ironically, he himself had designed improvements to the very gallows used for his execution.

Stevenson took this basic story and transformed it into a chilling examination of human psychology.

High Street

As you approach St Giles Cathedral, the Royal Mile becomes **High Street**. On the left you will find a statue of the philosopher and historian David Hume, depicted in a calm, thoughtful pose.

St Giles Cathedral ❻ (www.stgilescathedral.org.uk; May–Sept Mon–Fri 9am–7pm, Sat 9am–5pm, Sun 1–5am, Oct–Apr Mon–Sat 9am–5pm, Sun 1–5pm; free), on your right, was the original parish church for the city and has been at the centre of many of its most important developments. There has been a Christian place of worship on the site since the 9th century. Parts of the interior date back to 1100 and the crown spire is 500 years old; much of the exterior, however, is from the early 19th century.

The principal kirk of the Church of Scotland, St Giles was the church of John Knox, the Protestant reformer. From 1559 to 1572 his fiery Calvinist sermons influenced worshippers far beyond the cathedral walls and fuelled the religious discontent that split the population.

The small **Thistle Chapel** (built from 1909 to 1911) is dedicated to the Most Ancient and Most Noble Order of the Thistle, the highest order of chivalry in Scotland. The order was founded by James VII (James II of England) and continues today. There are a maximum of 16 knights at any one time, headed by the reigning monarch. Look up at the pinnacle of each seat and you'll see the carved and painted crests of the present members.

Groups of four visitors can climb the 91 steps to the

Stained glass by Edward Burne-Jones, St Giles Cathedral

rooftop for panoramic views and a 20-minute tour of the clock tower (book in advance).

Outside the cathedral in West Parliament Square you will find a statue of John Knox with Bible in hand. It was erected in 1906 not far from the reformer's supposed burial site. Look also for the heart-shaped stone mosaic worked into the cobbles, marking the site of the Edinburgh Tolbooth. The building collected city taxes during the 14th century but fulfilled several additional functions in later centuries. It was immortalised in Walter Scott's novel *The Heart of Midlothian* as a prison and place of execution. Passers-by traditionally spit on the cobbled heart to show their contempt.

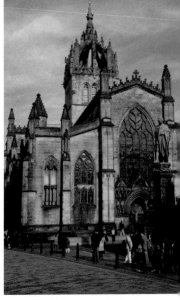

The kirk's west window is inspired by Robert Burns

Parliament Square is also home to **Parliament House**. After its construction in 1639, it held sessions of the Scottish Parliament until the 'Act of Union' in 1707, but since the 19th century it has been an integral part of the Scottish Law Courts. You'll see solicitors walking the alleyways and streets around the building, carrying briefs in hand and garbed in wigs and capes.

Just beyond the east side of the cathedral, topped by a small white unicorn, is the **Mercat Cross**. The first cross erected here, in the 14th century, marked the heart of the marketplace and provided a place for royal proclamations to be given a public hearing. It was also a place of execution. The present cross,

Britannica's home

To the right of the City Chambers, Anchor Close was once home to the printing works of William Smellie, editor and printer of the first edition of the Encyclopaedia Britannica, which appeared in 1768.

erected in 1756, is the starting point for many walking tours of the Old Town.

Across High Street you will find Edinburgh's **City Chambers**, housed here since 1811. The building itself was initially constructed to be a royal assembly for merchants, and an area of narrow streets and buildings was covered over and used as foundations. You can descend beneath today's street level and visit one of the 'real' Old Town streets at **The Real Mary King's Close** ❼ (entrance to the left of the City Chambers; www.realmarykings close.com; mid-Mar–Oct daily 10am–9pm, Nov–Mar Sun–Thu 10am–5pm, Fri–Sat 10am–9pm). Not for the claustrophobic, this tour is an excellent way of understanding what life was like for those who lived in labyrinth of narrow 'closes' that surrounded both sides of the High Street, where small, tightly packed dwellings saw almost no daylight and living conditions were squalid, cramped and plague-ridden.

Continuing down High Street, you will find **Moubray House** on the left. It is probably the oldest occupied dwelling in Edinburgh, recorded as far back as 1477. Next door is the **Scottish Storytelling Centre** (www.tracscotland. org; Mon–Sat 10am–6pm, July–Aug also Sun noon–6pm), a vibrant arts venue that celebrates Scotland's oral traditions, with live storytelling and theatre, and events such as the Scottish International Storytelling Festival in October each year. The centre incorporates a 99-seat auditorium downstairs and **John Knox House** ❽, which dates from 1490. Although it is doubtful the reformer ever lived here, evidence does suggest that he preached from the bow window. Opened as a museum in 1853, the small rooms display Knox memorabilia and the influential manuscripts from which he preached his Calvinist texts.

Directly across High Street from Knox House is the **Museum of Childhood ❾** (www.edinburghmuseums.org.uk; Mon–Sat 10am–5pm, Sun noon–5pm; free). Dedicated to games and toys of yesteryear, you'll find many amusing exhibits of street games, clockwork figures, dolls and teddy bears.

Canongate

The Royal Mile becomes **Canongate** at the point where it intersects St Mary's Street. This is the former boundary of the town of Edinburgh and the neighbouring town, called Canongate, which was a community of aristocrats and members of the royal court serving the Palace of Holyroodhouse. The two towns were united in 1856. Canongate derived its name from an edict by David I (1124–53), founder of the Abbey of Holyrood, who granted a right to raise a gate between the abbey and the Royal 'burgh' of Edinburgh.

Museum of Childhood

Several historic buildings lead off Canongate, and a number have interesting stories to tell. **Chessel's Court**, on the right, was the place where Deacon Brodie was finally caught in 1788. **Old Playhouse Close** was the site of a theatre where performances resulted in

John Knox House

so many riots that it was closed in 1769, after only 20 years. Dating from around 1625, **Moray House** saw a visit from Oliver Cromwell, Lord Protector of England; the house remained in the Moray family until the mid-19th century.

On the left as you walk, you will see the **Canongate Tolbooth ⑩**, with its distinctive clocktower overhanging the pavement. The building on the site dates from 1591 and served as a council chamber and courthouse for the town in addition to collecting tolls. Today the Tolbooth houses **The People's Story** (www.edinburghmuseums. org.uk; Mon–Sat 10am–5pm, also Sun during Aug noon–5pm; free), a museum charting the history of the ordinary citizens of Edinburgh from the 18th century to the present day. Reconstructions of townsfolk at home, at the pub, at high tea or in jail show how people lived in previous eras, augmented by written and oral testimonies.

Facing the Tolbooth is the **Museum of Edinburgh ⑪** (www.edinburghmuseums.org.uk; Mon–Sat 10am–5pm, also Sun in Aug noon–5pm; free), presenting local history exhibits from prehistoric times to the present. Huntly House, housing part of the museum, dates from the 16th century and houses treasures such as the collar and bowl of 'Greyfriars Bobby' (see page 58). The most exciting venture is 'Foundation – the

Story of a City', where Edinburgh literally grows below your feet in a blacked-out theatre.

Nearby **Canongate Kirk**  was built in 1688, and there are a number of significant figures interred in the peaceful churchyard, including the economist Adam Smith, the poet Robert Fergusson and Mrs Agnes McLehose (the 'Clarinda' of Burns' love poems). Just along from here is **Dunbar's Close Garden**, a pleasant little sun-trap.

Across the road and along Crichton's Close you will find the **Scottish Poetry Library** (www.spl.org.uk; Tue–Fri 10am–5pm, Thu until 7pm, Sat 10am–4pm; free), which gathers together contemporary and historic Scottish poetry in a smart modern building. Librarians will help you trace a half-remembered line of Burns or Fergusson.

As you approach the foot of Canongate, nip down **Reid's Close** to get a sneak preview of the Scottish Parliament Building. You'll see the MSP (Member of the Scottish Parliament) block; each member's office has a 'think pod' protruding from the wall. Back on Canongate, as the gates of the Palace of Holyroodhouse come into view, **White Horse Close** can be found on the left. This was the site of the White Horse Inn, the main coaching house at the end of the London–Edinburgh route.

Canongate Kirk

Holyrood

Cross the busy road at the bottom of Canongate to enter the **Holyrood** area, which comprises the palace, abbey and park, along with the Scottish Parliament building. The easternmost stretch of the Royal Mile – only 50 metres/yds long – is called Abbey Strand. It is flanked by a building that protected aristocratic debtors (known as the Abbey Lairds) from arrest and imprisonment; civil authorities had no jurisdiction within the Abbey grounds and could not enter to arrest them.

Palace of Holyroodhouse

The **Palace of Holyroodhouse** ⑱ (www.royalcollection.org. uk; daily Apr–Oct 9.30am–6pm; Nov–Mar 9.30am–4.30pm; free audio guide available; closed when royalty is in residence) is the official Scottish home of the reigning British monarch. It began life with a totally different purpose. In 1128 the king, David I, ceded land to the Augustinian order for the creation of the Abbey of Holyrood. He is said to have had a vision of the holy 'rood', or cross, between the antlers of a stag while hunting in this area.

The beautiful abbey was an important centre of worship but continued to have royal connections because of the surrounding hunting grounds. A guesthouse was built adjoining the abbey to be used as a base for royal hunting parties.

Scottish kings came to favour the site, and James IV decided to transform the simple lodgings into a true royal palace. In 1501 he had plans drawn up, which his son James V expanded after his death in 1513. In 1529 work started on a tower and royal apartments for James and his wife, Mary of Guise, which now constitute the western section and tower of the current palace. Mary, Queen of Scots, later occupied apartments here.

Over the next dozen decades, war and fire took their toll, and much rebuilding took place (the great tower, however, survived).

Following the return of the British monarchy in 1660, the palace buildings were refurbished and extended. Charles II never saw the palace on which he lavished so much money (the royal coffers expended £57,000, a fortune at the time), but he created the foundation of what we see today, with its amazing ornamental plaster work and carved wood panelling. His heir, James VI, lived at the castle in the 1680s, when the paint was barely dry.

During the 18th century Holyrood was neglected by succeeding British monarchs, who preferred to stay in their London residence, though Scottish noble families lived within the compound. It was not until 1822, when George IV made a state visit, that the fortunes of the palace revived. Since then, almost every reigning monarch has spent time (or held soirées) at Holyrood, and the palace has been carefully tended throughout the 20th century. The Queen usually spends time here in late June and early July.

The Scottish Parliament building

The Palace of Holyroodhouse

The **Great Stair** is the formal approach to the royal apartments in the southwestern tower. The plaster ceilings here date from 1678 and depict angels carrying the symbols of royal power: crown, sceptre, sword and wreath of laurel leaves. The **Royal Dining Room** is situated at the top of the Great Stair. This majestic room is used for modern-day entertaining when the Queen hosts dinners and banquets. On the walls are portraits of Bonnie Prince Charlie and his brother, Prince Henry.

The **Throne Room** is one of a series of apartments built during the reign of Charles II, though it was originally designed as a guard room that screened entrants to the private chambers beyond. The thrones on view here date from a visit by George V and Queen Mary in 1927.

Two magnificent state rooms follow, both designed by Sir William Bruce as part of the extensions and refurbishment in the 1660s. The **Evening and Morning Drawing Rooms** (originally the Presence Chamber and the Privy Chamber) were designed to meet visiting dignitaries and are splendid in their detail; the oak-panelled ceiling is superbly decorated. Be sure to take a look at the painting above the mantel. The scene, depicting Cupid and Psyche, was considered too risqué for the eyes of Queen Victoria, and during her reign it was covered by a mirror. The **King's Antechamber** was where he entertained his more favoured guests.

The King's Bedchamber is perhaps the most richly decorated room in the royal apartments. Adorning the walls are 17th-century tapestries depicting heroic scenes from the life of Alexander the Great. Although the bed dates from the 1680s, it has never been slept in by royalty. It belongs to the Hamilton family, who have served as hereditary keepers of the palace. Beyond is the King's Closet, where only his intimate entourage would be admitted for evenings of drinking and card games.

From the king's apartments you will enter the **Great Gallery**, a long room that is home to 111 portraits of Scottish rulers dating back to antiquity. Commissioned by Charles II, the paintings were all the work of one man, Dutch artist Jacob de Wit. He worked from likenesses of actual monarchs to produce his portraits. For ancient or legendary kings such as Fergus – who was said to have been related to the Pharaohs of Egypt – fashionable imagery of the time helped to create the finished figures. De Wit was paid a reasonable stipend of £120 per year to produce the works, examples of which can also be seen in other rooms of the palace.

The Great Stair

The oldest part of the palace, the **James V Tower** (once called the Great Tower), is for many the highlight of the tour. Its stone walls, which survived both fires in the 16th century, sheltered rooms occupied by Mary Stuart and her second husband, Lord Darnley, in the 1560s. On the third floor is the **Bed Chamber of Mary, Queen of Scots**, with her antechambers surrounding it. Stairs connect her room to that occupied by her husband.

Nearby is the **Outer Chamber of Mary, Queen of Scots**, where she socialised with her favourites and debated religion with John Knox. It is also where her secretary, David Rizzio, was left to bleed to death after being stabbed by Lord Darnley and his cronies; a bronze plaque marks the spot. You will find a number of Mary's personal effects on display. The chambers were totally refurbished by Charles II, including larger windows to balance the design of the new extensions. However, the original ceiling of Mary's bedchamber is still in place.

Outside by the entrance, more precious artworks are on view in the Queen's Gallery. Also set in manicured gardens, are the remains of **Holyrood Abbey**. Today, it comprises little more than the walls of the church nave. The rest of the abbey was razed to the ground in 1570, but the church was saved because it was a parish church and therefore served the local community. Ornate carvings on the stone facade can still just be discerned. A small stone tomb in the southeast corner houses the bones of several members of the royal family. Originally, these all had separate burial sites, but they were sacked by religious protesters. Queen Victoria arranged for the bones of David II, James II, James V and Lord Darnley to be re-interred in a common tomb.

Queen's Gallery

The Queen's Gallery, (same opening times as palace) in front of the palace, features changing exhibits from the priceless royal art collection. Monarchists will adore the shop, which is adjoined by a café.

Arthur's Seat

Holyrood Park and Arthur's Seat

To the south of the palace are the green landscapes of **Holyrood Park**, including the volcanic peak known as Arthur's Seat. Once royal hunting grounds, today these areas are used for open-air events, concerts and fireworks displays. On sunny days this is an ideal family picnic spot. The rugged peak of **Arthur's Seat** ⑭, 823ft (251 metres) in height, can be reached by footpaths all around its base. The path nearest the palace takes walkers along the base of **Salisbury Crags**, a volcanic ridge. The vantage point at the summit of Arthur's Seat offers wonderful views of the city and across the Firth of Forth to the north.

On the far side of Arthur's Seat is **Duddingston Loch**, a bird sanctuary. **Duddingston Kirk**, near the banks of the loch, is one of the oldest Scottish churches still in regular use, founded in the 12th century. A watchtower was erected in the early 1800s to deter body snatchers. On the causeway leading off

The Debating Chamber is at the heart of parliament

Old Church Lane is **Prince Charlie's Cottage**, where the 'Young Pretender' stayed in 1745 while planning his strategy to defeat the English and retake the British throne.

The Scottish Parliament

Back in Holyrood, the **Scottish Parliament Building ⓯** (tel: 0131 348 5200; www.scottish.parliament.uk; Mon–Sat subject to Parliamentary business; tours free, booking essential) is the home of Scotland's devolved democracy. In this sprawling complex of seven buildings Members of the Scottish Parliament (or MSPs) question the First Minister and his cabinet, and legislate on health, education and other domestic matters. If you wish to see Parliament at work, visit on a business day and attend a Committee meeting or a parliamentary debate (ticket required, free). Visitors are welcome to explore all public areas without booking a tour.

Directly in front of Parliament, on Holyrood Road, is **Our Dynamic Earth ⓰** (www.dynamicearth.co.uk; Apr–Oct daily 10am–5.30pm, July–Aug until 6pm, Nov–Mar Wed–Sun 10am–5.30pm), a futuristic building under a brilliant white-tented roof. This is an interactive journey through the history of the Earth from the moment of the 'Big Bang'. Using the latest technology, the exhibits are entertaining and educational for all ages, posing questions about our roles as managers of the Earth's resources and the planet's future. The fun parts include getting to touch an iceberg, experiencing the effects of a bubbling volcano and witnessing a crash landing in the rainforest. The tour de force is the 3D cinema that delivers amazing 4D effects that allow you to touch, feel and smell the experience as you journey across the globe; it even snows on the audience.

Building the Scottish Parliament

In a referendum of 1997, the Scots voted overwhelmingly for devolution. Donald Dewar, then Scottish Secretary, chose the site of a former brewery for the new parliament and ensured that Catalan architect Enric Miralles won the 1999 competition to design the building. A year later, both Dewer and Miralles had died, leaving the Scottish civil service to grapple with the project's administration, and Miralles' architectural firm to puzzle over his sketches.

Six years and a budget-busting £500 million later, the building was finished. Some love it, some hate it. What is largely agreed is that the interior of the building far outstrips the exterior. Despite the considerable use of concrete and granite, Miralles intended the parliament complex to resemble a plant. Each of the seven buildings forms a leaf of the plant, connected at the centre by the Garden Lobby. Leaf-shaped skylights allow daylight to illuminate the activity of the MSPs in the lobby, who pause here for a drink or to be interviewed by journalists at the foot of the staircase leading to the Debating Chamber. Be sure to visit the chamber, whether or not a debate is in session. The ceiling is a marvel – roof beams are held up by 112 steel nodes, all of different sizes. Look out too for bottle-shaped cut-outs on the west wall – symbolising not whisky bottles, rather the people of Scotland looking in on the work of Parliament.

Despite the Scottish Parliament Building's controversial aspects, it is remarkably accessible to the visiting public. And even on a gloomy day the building is infused with light, accentuating the feeling of open government.

Outdoor drinking and markets in Grassmarket

Grassmarket and Greyfriars

In the shadows of the southern walls of Edinburgh Castle lies the rectangular space of **Grassmarket**. From 1477 this was a marketplace for local farmers as well as one of the main sites for executions. Huge crowds would gather for the gory events – as they did for the markets – and a series of hostelries and pubs set up business to cater for them. Some still operate, putting out tables in summer so you can enjoy al fresco food and drinks. At the eastern end of Grassmarket there is a memorial to the Covenanters (Scottish Protestant clergymen) martyred by Catholic Stuart kings in the 17th century.

From Grassmarket, **Cowgate** runs parallel to the Royal Mile to Holyrood on a lower level. The road has a number of bridges spanning its route, creating a shadowy, dark and almost sombre appearance. The alleyways and passages leading off this thoroughfare are some of the oldest in the city. Sadly, a fire destroyed a large chunk of the central passage in 2002.

Cowgate was known for generations as the Irish Quarter because many families came here to escape the potato famine in their own country. At the western end (where Cowgate meets Holyrood Road), you will see one of the few remaining sections of the **Flodden Wall**, which was begun after the Scottish defeat at the Battle of Flodden in 1513.

West Bow and **Candlemaker Row** are streets leading away from Cowgate Head and the east end of Grassmarket. Here you'll find interesting shops for antiques, collectibles, comestibles and antiquarian books. Both these streets lead to the upper level of the George IV Bridge.

From Candlemakers Row, enter the Greyfriars Churchyard through a gate on the right. The **Greyfriars Church** ⓱ was closely linked with the Protestant Covenanters, and many of those hanged in the Grassmarket are buried here. The church was opened in 1620 and the National Covenant was signed here in 1638. The church became a barracks during Oliver Cromwell's occupation of the city in the 1650s; in 1718 there was an explosion of gunpowder that had been stored in the tower. Fire did further damage in 1845. Greyfriars Church was restored in 1938 to produce the building you see now.

The **graveyard** has some ornate tombs, with skulls, crossbones and other symbols of death. Gravestones rest along the tenement walls marking the outer perimeter. Among those buried here are George Buchanan, tutor to Mary, Queen of Scots; James Craig, architect of Edinburgh's New Town; and Joseph Black, physicist and

Greyfriars Bobby

chemist. Just beside the main entrance is the grave of Greyfriars Bobby. From here you can see some of the best views of the layout of the Old Town, with layer upon layer of crenulated rooftops and hundreds of chimney stacks.

The main gate of the churchyard leads out to Greyfriars Place, and across the street you will find an excellent view of the **National Museum of Scotland** ⓲ (www.nms.ac.uk; daily 10am–5pm; free). With its main entrance on Chambers Street, the museum is housed in a remarkable building designed by architects Benson and Forsyth. It charts the history of Scotland, bringing under one roof a number of important collections of artefacts. The story begins 3.4 billion years ago with displays of fossils and rock, marking the geological changes that forged the landscape. It continues through the turbulent eras of Scottish history, and on to the industrial developments of modern times.

Greyfriars Bobby

One of the most famous inhabitants of Edinburgh, Greyfriars Bobby was a Skye terrier belonging to 'Auld Jock' Gray, a local police constable. When Jock died in 1858, Bobby followed the funeral procession to the graveyard at Greyfriars Church and then stayed at his master's grave for the next 14 years, leaving it only to look for food at the nearby tavern.

Though he was legally a stray and thus under threat of being destroyed, the whole city rallied around the faithful dog. The Lord Provost issued a licence that allowed Bobby to maintain his vigil, which he did until his death in 1873. He was buried in the graveyard, and a statue, financed by public donations, was erected outside the tavern. Bobby's collar and bowl can be seen at the Museum of Edinburgh, and his story has been told in a Walt Disney movie and a feature film starring Christopher Lee.

The main hall of the Grand Gallery, augmented by its towering pillars, would provide an impressive place to start any museum visit. Light pours through the high windows, enhancing the objects on display in this extraordinary collection. Of particular note here is the Millennium clock that, every hour on the hour, delights with its music and light performance as the figures comes to life.

National Museum of Scotland

Look through the arch at the eastern end of the Grand Gallery and you'll see a Tyrannosaurus rex guarding a stunning series of galleries about the Natural World. Beyond here, various other galleries allow you to travel through the country's history, explore ideas and inventions from some of Scotland's finest innovators and gain an insight into world cultures.

Currently around half of the Post Modernist 1998 building is closed due to another exciting project that will provide ten more galleries in which to showcase the collections of decorative art, design, fashion, science and technology.

Other facilities include three shops, the informal Balcony Café and the Tower Restaurant (see page 110), which offers panoramic views over the city skyline and superlative food.

The National Museum of Scotland is at the heart of the old **University of Edinburgh** quarter whose students still attend lectures in the nearby sandstone buildings. The university's Old College building holds the **Talbot Rice Gallery** 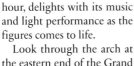 (tel: 0131 650 2210; Tue–Fri 10am–5pm, Sat noon–5pm; free).

Here contemporary visual art is displayed in the White Gallery, while the Georgian Gallery, designed by William Playfair, exhibits the university's collection of Old Master paintings, sculptures and Renaissance bronzes.

The city has a reputation for research and development in medicine, which began in 1505 with the founding of, what would become, the Royal College of Surgeons, followed by the Royal College of Physicians in 1681 and the School of Medicine a few years later. You can probe further into the city's medical history at the **Surgeons' Hall Museum** [20] (www.museum.rcsed.ac.uk; closed for redevelopment until summer 2015), on Nicolson Street. Also on Nicolson Street is the **Edinburgh Festival Theatre** (see page 88).

Although the university campus has grown, with sites across the city, the streets here have inexpensive eateries, with an eclectic range of shops selling clothes, music and books.

View across New Town

South of the museums, a short walk down Forest Road and with its entrance on Lauriston Place, stands the ornate **George Heriot's School**. Although not open to the public, its towers and beautifully carved stone walls can be seen from various vantage points in the city. 'Jinglin' Geordie' Heriot was a banker, goldsmith and

jeweller to James IV. When he died in 1624, his fortune was bequeathed to the education and upkeep of orphans, and the school was built for this purpose.

THE NEW TOWN

By the beginning of the 18th century, life in the city of Edinburgh (today's Old Town) was overcrowded and unsanitary. The city had grown very little since the 14th century, yet its population was said to be over 50,000. Large families lived in high tenements, sharing a well with hundreds of other families. Sewage and dirty water were thrown from upper floors to the streets below and left to fester.

In 1725 the Lord Provost of the city, George Drummond, first raised the possibility of expansion to the northeast, across what was called Barefoot's Parks to the green fields beyond. His ideas were not made official until 1752, and it was another 14 years before plans were put into place for a competition to create a design for this new development, to be called the **New Town**.

There were logistical problems to be overcome. At the foot of the castle was Nor' Loch, a large expanse of water that required draining. There would also have to be adequate access between the older and newer parts of town, including a bridge over the valley between Barefoot's Parks and the Royal Mile.

The competition winner, announced in 1766, was James Craig, an unknown 23-year-old architect and native of the city. His plan was a simple grid: a symmetrical design with straight streets and grand squares. The recent union with England was the inspiration for street names such as 'Rose' and 'Thistle'. The royal family was honoured with George Street, Queen Street and Princes Street. Surprisingly, the plan contained little detail for the buildings to line the streets and frame the squares. Instead, Craig concentrated on the overall design.

In 1763 construction had already begun on North Bridge, which would provide access from the Old Town. Nor' Loch was drained (creating land for today's Princes Street Gardens), and the Mound was constructed to provide a second, westerly access between the two settlements.

The first houses built here did not adhere to any set design. In 1782, after only a few years, the city decided to impose planning guidelines. At the same time, an architect named Robert Adam became popular in the fashionable circles of the well-to-do, having made a name for himself in England. It was he who would add the 'flesh' of handsome buildings to the 'bones' of Craig's design.

Georgian architecture

Today, the streets of the New Town have perhaps the greatest collection of Georgian architecture in the world. Together with the Old Town, the New Town is a Unesco World Heritage Site, safeguarding its special character.

By the beginning of the 19th century, the New Town had become so popular that plans were made for a second stage. This would be a largely residential area extending north from Queen Street, incorporating a number of roundabouts (circuses) as well as straight roads. Most influential at this stage was architect William Playfair, and his flair can be seen in many of the streets and public buildings of the time. These streets are still largely residential and make an interesting area to explore, displaying an abundance of original detail. Edinburgh became known as the 'Athens of the North' for both its aesthetic beauty and its wealth of talented artists, philosophers and scientists. Because so many buildings are still used as residences, there are relatively few attractions to visit compared with the Old Town.

Stores on Princes Street

Princes Street

Looking north from the high ground of the Old Town, the first street you can see is **Princes Street**. It was once regarded as the most beautiful street in Europe, a claim that is difficult to appreciate today since so many of the original buildings have been replaced. The long-awaited completion of the tramline has fuelled a surge in investment in Princes Street and bought a fresh feel to what is considered Scotland's Oxford Street. There are splendid views of the castle all along its length.

On the south side of the street – in the open ground below the castle and on the site of the formerly marshy Nor' Loch – are **Princes Street Gardens**, a welcome place to relax on a

The National Gallery of Scotland

sunny day. The West Gardens have a number of interesting memorial statues and sculptures, including the **Scottish American War Memorial** (World War I) and the **Royal Scots Memorial**.

At the centre of the gardens is the **Ross Open Air Theatre** (for show times tel: 0131 221 6335), which plays host to free concerts throughout the year, particularly during the festival season. During the summer, beside the flight of steps carrying people up to the Mound, you will find the **Floral Clock** ㉑. Planted with hundreds of pretty blooms, all in pristine condition, it has kept accurate time since its creation in 1903.

The West and East Gardens are split by the **Mound**, an artificial slope of rock and soil that carries a road connecting the New Town with the Old. Here you will find two of the most important galleries in the city, housed in classical buildings designed by Playfair and connected by the Weston Link. Set back from Princes Street is the **Scottish National Gallery** ㉒ (www.nationalgalleries.org; daily 10am–6pm, Thu until 7pm; free), opened in 1859, which houses a collection of works by native Scottish artists and international masters. The collection – and indeed the building itself – is not huge or overbearing; allowing visitors to relax and enjoy the art perhaps more than is possible in such massive galleries as the Louvre or Rijksmuseum. What it lacks in size, the gallery makes up for in quality. Raphael's *Bridgewater Madonna*, a Rembrandt *Self-Portrait Aged 51* and Velázquez's *An Old Woman Cooking Eggs* are only three from a collection that includes pieces by Titian, Rubens, Constable, Turner, Monet and Van Gogh. Scottish artists include Allan Ramsay, Sir Henry Raeburn and Sir David Wilkie.

The £30-million **Weston Link** is a huge underground passage that burrows through the Mound and connects the Scottish National Gallery with the Royal Scottish Academy. Visitor facilities here include a 200-seat lecture theatre (free lunchtime lectures are given by gallery experts), touch-screen displays to explore the collections, and a garden-side café and restaurant.

Designed almost as the Scottish National Gallery's twin, the **Royal Scottish Academy** ㉓ holds regular exhibitions of Scottish and international art, and displays by its members.

The castle viewed from Princes Street Gardens

Between the two buildings, **East Princes Gardens** are smaller than the West Gardens. As part of the Hogmanay celebrations an ice rink covers the lawns, where you can enjoy outdoor skating in a picturesque setting for a few weeks. Rising above the flower beds is the solemn **Scott Monument** ㉔ (www. edinburghmuseums.org.uk; Apr–Sept daily 10am–7pm, Oct–Mar until 4pm), a huge, stone neo-Gothic structure with four buttresses supporting a spire. The whole edifice is 200ft (61 metres)

The Scott Monument

high. Within sits the statue of novelist Sir Walter Scott (and his faithful dog, Maida) carved from Cararra marble. Designed by George Meikle Kemp, a self-taught draughtsman of humble birth, the monument took its inspiration from the design of Melrose Abbey, which lies south of Edinburgh in the Borders. Carved into the structure are 64 statuettes representing characters from Scott's books. Steps (287 in all) inside, the outer columns lead up to galleries at four levels. The **view** from the topmost gallery is spectacular.

Beyond the monument is Waverley Bridge. Here you can board buses for a tour of city attractions. This is also the site of **Waverley Station**, and the sound of arriving trains can be heard as background noise throughout the day. The lines take a dramatic route via ditches cut through Princes Street Gardens and under the Mound (in the National Gallery you can feel a faint movement as the trains travel underneath). Princes Mall, which sits on the corner of Princes Street, is where you will find the city's main **Tourist Information Office** (see page 133).

On the south side of the station is Market Street, which was one of the principal market sites during the Victorian era. Market Street is home to the **Edinburgh City Art Centre** (www.edinburghmuseums.org.uk; Mon–Sat 10am–5pm, Sun noon–5pm; free), showcasing the work of up-and-coming artists. On the same street you will also find the ticket office for the Military Tattoo (see also page 35).

At the eastern end of Princes Street is **General Register House**, completed in 1788 from a design by Robert Adam. As part of the **National Records of Scotland** (www. nrscotland.gov.uk), it stores historical records, such as those created by Scottish government, businesses, landed estates, families, courts and churches. Behind is **New Register House**, which stores records of births, marriages and deaths in Scotland, while in front is a statue of the Duke of Wellington, resplendent in battle dress astride his steed, Copenhagen.

George Street

The centrepiece of Craig's original design for the New Town was **George Street**. The grand thoroughfare, anchored at each end by a large square, had a symmetrical pattern of streets on both its flanks. George Street was the traditional centre of Edinburgh's financial district, where many

Secret Gardens

Like many cities, Edinburgh has picturesque gardens among its paved streets and rows of houses. Unlike most other cities, however, many of these gardens are private and enjoyed by only a favoured few.

When the New Town was planned in the 1760s, it incorporated squares (such as St Andrew) and green spaces (such as Queen Street Gardens) as an integral part of the design. The gardens were held in common by the householders who lived around them, with each household having a key to gain access through locked, wrought-iron gates.

The rights and responsibilities of the 'keyholders' have been passed down through the generations, and today these gates are still locked to the general public. The fine statues and manicured lawns may be viewed from the outside only.

Georgian House

successful bankers increased the wealth of their trusting investors. Scottish banking has long been held in high regard and still plays an important part in the financial world. However, the buildings – beautiful though they are – have not been able to accommodate modern computerised banking equipment; and many institutions have moved to modern buildings around the city. This hasn't made George Street an empty shell. Where the banks have moved out, fashionable shops, bars and restaurants have moved in.

The western end of George Street begins at **Charlotte Square** ㉕, originally named St George's Square after England's patron saint (mirroring St Andrew Square at the street's eastern end). The name was changed to honour Queen Charlotte – George III's wife – who felt a little upset at having been left out of the original plans. After all, her husband and two sons had roads named after them: George Street and Princes Street.

Charlotte Square is arguably the jewel of the New Town. The facades of elegant houses on the north side were designed by Robert Adam and have changed little since they were finished in 1805. In the centre of the terrace is **Georgian House** (daily Apr–Oct 10am–5pm, July–Aug until 6pm; Mar, Nov 11am–4pm), owned by the National Trust for Scotland and restored in period style to show the workings of a typical Georgian household; even the floorboards have been dry scrubbed in the original manner. All of the many items in the house are authentic, including a huge array of kitchen utensils, furniture, carpets and curtains. Curiously, the bedchamber is on the ground floor; upper-floor bedrooms became fashionable at a later date. The basement kitchen is a masterpiece of late 18th-century domestic technology.

On the western flank of the square, **West Register House**, designed originally by Robert Reid in 1811 as a church (St George's), was taken over by the government in 1960 and is now part of the **National Records of Scotland**. The building at the corner of Charlotte Square and South Charlotte Street was the birthplace of Alexander Graham Bell, inventor of the telephone.

Heading east along George Street you will pass the 19th-century **Assembly Rooms**. With their magnificent

Scottish National Portrait Gallery

Bank of Scotland

The Scots have always been among the modern world's most successful bankers, and Edinburgh is one of Europe's biggest financial centres. Unlike their English counterparts, three Scottish clearing banks retain the right to print their own distinctive banknotes.

chandeliers, the rooms have been the setting for many great social occasions and are used as a venue for the Festival Fringe. Across the road is the **Church of St Andrew and St George** ㉖ (1785), whose oval-shaped interior witnessed the 'Great Disruption' of 1843. At the far end of George Street, the most stunning building on **St Andrew Square** is that belonging to the **Royal Bank of Scotland**. Originally a house, it was designed by Sir William Chambers and completed in 1772; the dome was added in 1858.

Scottish National Portrait Gallery

From St Andrew Square, it is only a short walk north to Queen Street, where you will find the **Scottish National Portrait Gallery** ㉗ (www.nationalgalleries.org; daily 10am–5pm, Thu until 7pm; free) on the corner. More than 200 paintings of famous – and infamous – Scots can be found in the collection, which was initiated by David, 11th Earl of Buchan. Following the earl's death, Scottish historian Thomas Carlyle decided to inspire his fellow countrymen through a national gallery devoted to their heroes. He obtained private backing for the creation of the gallery, which opened in 1889.

Designed by Sir Robert Rowand Anderson, the building was constructed in neo-Gothic style, with statues on the outer facade depicting Scottish poets, artists and statesmen. The entrance (Great Hall) also portrays famous Scots in a beautifully detailed frieze just below the cornice; it's a veritable 'Who's Who' of the Scottish establishment. The Great Hall is also home to several sculptures, including one of Carlyle, the gallery's founding father.

A glass lift ascends to the top floor where the beautifully restored galleries allow natural light into the room from above. Exhibits, which change on a regular basis, bring to life some of the great individuals who have made their mark on Scottish history, from Mary, Queen of Scots and Robert Burns to more recent legends in sport and the arts, such as Manchester United's manager Sir Alex Ferguson and comedian Billy Connolly. Thematic short-term exhibitions such as Remembering the First World War draw on the collection to highlight the people of Scotland's impact on world events. Likenesses can be found on canvas, as prints and photographs, or as sculptures.

National Monument, Calton Hill

Further changing displays can be seen in the new Photography Gallery and you can find more about the collection in the interactive Touchscreen Gallery.

Calton Hill

From the eastern end of Princes Street, the eye is drawn to a hill topped with a series of intriguing, disparate buildings. This is **Calton Hill** ㉘, built around 328ft (100 metres) of hard volcanic rock. Its monuments and architecture are said to have been another contributor to Edinburgh's epithet 'Athens of the North'. You will be met by a flight of steep steps, but the superb views across the city make the climb worthwhile.

At the hill's crest, you will find the **City Observatory** complex (being redeveloped as an arts centre and due to open to the public for the first time in 2016). The Old Observatory here is the only building designed by James Craig left in the city (completed in 1792). Playfair's New Observatory was built in 1818 and granted Royal Observatory status in 1822, although the smoky skies and train steam over the city made it an unsuitable location for watching the stars. The Royal Observatory was eventually relocated to Blackford Hill, further south, in 1895.

The nearby **Nelson Monument** (www.edinburgh museums.org.uk; Apr–Sept Mon–Sat 10am–7pm, Sun noon–5pm, Oct–Mar Mon–Sat 10am–3pm), an elegant tower 98ft (30 metres) high, commemorates the naval victory at Trafalgar in 1805. You can climb the column for panoramic views of the city and the Firth of Forth to the north. At the top of the tower is a white ball on a metal stake. As one o'clock approaches, the ball rises to the top of the stake and then drops exactly on the stroke of one. This device is a visual counterpart to the firing of the One O'Clock Gun at the Castle. It could easily be seen by ships in the Firth of Forth and was a useful safeguard if prevailing winds carried the sound of the gunfire the wrong way.

A colonnaded circular monument to the right was raised in the memory of Dugald Stewart, professor of moral philosophy at the University of Edinburgh in the 1780s. The classical design was taken from examples in Athens.

The most fascinating structure on Calton Hill is the **National Monument**. What looks from a distance like a huge Greek temple with many Doric columns turns out to

Dean Village and the Water of Leith

be only a single facade with 12 columns. It was planned in the 1820s as a symbol of Scottish national pride and designed as a mini-Parthenon, in deference to the neoclassical style popular at the time. Unfortunately, the public was not enthusiastic, the funding ran out and the project was abandoned, giving the monument its other name: 'Scotland's Disgrace'.

EDINBURGH'S VILLAGES

Edinburgh has throughout most of its history been a very compact city. Even the New Town had very set boundaries. The entire city was surrounded by open countryside with a scattering of small villages. But massive growth during the 20th century saw Edinburgh absorb many of these formerly independent communities into its ever-enlarging limits. Surprisingly – and happily – the villages did not allow their character to be diluted and swallowed up into one homogenous suburb. They still maintain their own individual charms and are an important element in Edinburgh's continuing appeal.

Dean Village

Less than half a mile (0.8km) from the western end of Princes Street is **Dean Village** ㉙, which straddles the ribbon-thin Water of Leith, whose narrow valley drops steeply here. Dean Bridge carries the main road over the Water; it was designed and built by Thomas Telford, one of Scotland's greatest civil engineers.

Dean was an industrial village, its economy depending on numerous small mills that have now completely disappeared. A walk beside the Water offers the most interesting views, so don't cross the bridge. Instead, take the cobbled alley of Bells Brae to Hawthornbank Road down into the valley. You'll find great views of the rear of the Georgian houses of the New Town as well as the small cottages of Dean Village itself.

A 10-minute walk east on Belford Road brings you to the **Scottish National Gallery of Modern Art** ㉚ (www.nationalgalleries.org; daily 10am–5pm, Aug until 6pm; free), founded in 1959. Scotland's national collection of modern and contemporary art is housed in two neo-classical buildings, Modern One and Modern Two, set in parkland dotted with sculptures by important artists like Ian Henry Moore and Nathan Coley.

Modern One features works from French and Russian art from the beginning of the 20th century, cubist paintings and expressionist and modern British art – highlights include paintings by Matisse and Picasso. The Gallery also houses a remarkable collection of art produced since World War II, as well as a superb collection of modern Scottish art. Art by

Francis Bacon, David Hockney and Andy Warhol sit alongside more recent works by Damien Hirst and Tracey Emin.

Occupying a fine Victorian mansion, **Modern Two** ⑪ (former Dean Gallery) is home to a changing programme of exhibitions and displays drawn from the permanent collection. On permanent display is a fascinating recreation of Eduard Paolozzi's studio, as well as his huge sculpture, Vulcan, that dominates the café.

Inverleith

Immediately north of Edinburgh's New Town is **Inverleith**, an area full of green sites. Large schools with acres of grounds, playing fields and recreation areas are interspersed with sumptuous houses set in leafy lanes. It was here that the **Royal Botanic Garden** ㉜ (www.rbge.org.uk; daily 10am–dusk; free, charge for glasshouse) was moved in 1823 from a location

Scottish National Gallery of Modern Art

The Temperate Palm House, Royal Botanic Garden

not far from the Abbey of Holyrood. The garden had been founded as early as 1670 as a resource for medical research, affiliated for many years with the Royal College of Physicians.

The present site covers 70 acres (28 hectares) of ground divided into several different natural environments. The huge Victorian glasshouse, the Temperate Palm House, is impressive and packed with ferns and palms that thrive in the warm, damp environment. A large 1960s glasshouse sits beside it and, though lacking the elegance of its neighbour, still boasts an impressive collection. The surrounding landscaped grounds are kept in pristine condition. Mature trees shade lawns and flower beds that are home to numerous bird species and cheeky grey squirrels. You can also wander through the soothing Chinese garden, with its waterfalls and pretty red pergola.

Corstorphine

About 3 miles (5km) west of Edinburgh's centre, past the rugby ground at Murrayfield, you will find **Corstorphine**. For centuries this was a farming village, separated from the city by the green expanse of Corstorphine Hill. **Edinburgh Zoo** ❸ (www.edinburghzoo.org.uk; daily Apr–Sept 9am–6pm, Mar and Oct until 5pm, Nov–Feb until 4.30pm) is spread out across the hillside with visitors needing to climb some inclines to the upper enclosures.

The zoo opened in 1913 and was designed with enclosures rather than cages, a new idea at the time. This offered a more natural habitat for animals and a clearer view for visitors. When the zoo celebrated the first successful hatching in captivity of a king penguin in 1919, it gained world renown: no other zoo had examples of this penguin species.

Today, Edinburgh Zoo continues work on the conservation of animal species and acts as an educational resource. The zoo has the world's largest outdoor penguin pool – don't miss the Penguin Parade (daily at 2.15pm). There are over 127 species of animals on view here, including endangered rhinos, beautiful big cats and herds of antelope and zebra.

Amid great excitement, in 2011 Edinburgh Zoo welcomed a breeding pair of giant pandas (Tian Tian and Yang Guang) on loan from China, and the only giant pandas living in the UK. The Panda Experience (free) is a major attraction and viewing slots are limited so book in advance.

The Signal Tower, Leith

Leith

Situated on the coast, **Leith 34** is 3 miles (5km) from the city centre. It has been an important settlement since the 14th century and was the largest port in Scotland for many years, handling Edinburgh's cargo. It was a fiercely independent settlement with its own fishing fleet and shipbuilding industry. In 1920 Leith was incorporated into the city of Edinburgh.

After a brief 20th-century decline, Leith's fortunes have revived. The old warehouses have been transformed into upmarket apartments and fashionable office buildings, and there is a buzz of chic commercial activity that has spawned smart restaurants and bars. Local authorities have restored some of Leith's handsome commercial buildings, such as the grand **Custom House**, the **Corn Exchange** and **Leith Assembly Rooms**. Older locals – trawler men or dock-workers – might lament the loss of Leith's gritty, salt-of-the-earth reputation, but the town has an air of excitement about it. Buses from the city centre will carry you here in minutes.

Royal Yacht Britannia

Situated in the **Ocean Terminal** leisure and shopping complex (designed by Sir Terence Conran) is the **Royal Yacht *Britannia*** ③⑤ (www.royalyachtbritannia. co.uk; visitor centre and yacht: daily July–Sept 9.30am–4.30pm, Apr–June and Oct until 4pm, Nov–Mar 10am–3.30pm; booking advisable). Decommissioned in 1997, the yacht once transported the Queen and her official representatives on 968 royal and diplomatic visits to venues around the world.

The 412ft (125-metre) three-masted ship was

launched in April 1953, when Elizabeth II was in the first few months of her reign. *Britannia* travelled all over the world, entertaining princes, presidents and diplomats. But she is perhaps best remembered as the royal honeymoon boat. Princess Margaret began the tradition, to be followed by three of the Queen's children: Anne, Andrew and Charles, who journeyed with the newly designated Diana, Princess of Wales, around the Mediterranean in 1981.

A visitor centre introduces the yacht, its crew and the royal patrons, and on board you can see the royal apartments (designed by Sir Hugh Casson in the style of an English country house), grand dining room, Admiral's quarters and engine room.

The most attractive part of Leith is the **Shore**, a short walk east of *Britannia*. The Shore formed around the mouth of the Water of Leith, the narrow river running through Edinburgh. Even here the Water is really little more than a large stream, but it flows into the Firth of Forth and beyond into the North Sea. The Shore comprises a quayside and several cobbled lanes with restaurants where you can have a pleasant lunch. The surrounding warehouse districts have interesting souvenir stores. A little way to the south are **Leith Links**, said to be the birthplace of golf, where the Honourable Company of Edinburgh Golfers built a clubhouse in 1767, now a public park with tree-lined walkways and a venue for the Edinburgh Mela Festival (see page 96).

Cramond

At present-day **Cramond** ㊱, located at the mouth of the River Almond, the Romans constructed a fort in the 2nd century AD at the eastern end of their defensive Antonine Wall. The foundations of the fort can still be seen, and artefacts from the site are found in the Museum of Edinburgh (see page 46).

Looking across the causeway to Cramond Island

Sailing boats and small pleasure craft dock at Cramond, where the tidal river exits into the Firth of Forth. Much of the village is from the 18th century, and the whitewashed cottages are very picturesque. There are pleasant walks along the coastline and you can stop for a drink at the Cramond Inn, believed to be a setting described in Stevenson's St Ives.

EXCURSIONS

An effortless day's outing from the capital brings you within reach of much of Scotland's past and present and the forces that have shaped the country: its critical topography, its dominant families and its gifted architects.

South Queensferry and the Forth Bridges

Approximately 8 miles (13km) west of the city is **South Queensferry** ③, a town that developed as a crossing point of the Forth for routes to the north of Scotland. It is said that Queen Margaret, later St Margaret, often travelled this route in the late 11th century and that the town took its name from her journeys. A plaque on the water's edge at the Binks (a natural jetty formed by a rocky outcrop) marks her landing site.

The Victorian solution for crossing the Forth resulted in one of the greatest engineering achievements of the era, the **Forth Bridge**. Completed in 1890, the bridge comprises three huge cantilevers joined by two suspended spans, for a total length of 4,746ft (1,447 metres). For many years it was the longest bridge in the world, overshadowing the town which sits on the banks of the river below. Maintenance is a mammoth task, and painters work constantly on the structure.

In 1964 a sister structure, the **Forth Road Bridge**, was completed to take vehicular traffic across the Firth. The bridge is a single, unsupported span 3,300ft (1,006 metres) in length. Pictures of the building of both bridges can be found in the town museum on High Street.

From a small jetty below the railway bridge, you can take a ferry out into the Firth of Forth to tiny **Inchcolm Island** ❸❽ (www.maidoftheforth.co.uk; sailings most days June–Aug, less frequent Apr–May and Sept–Oct). Here lies the ruined Abbey of St Colm, founded in the 12th century and named after St Columba, who had brought Christianity to western Scotland 600 years earlier.

The Forth Bridge

Linlithgow Palace

Hopetoun House and Linlithgow Palace

Situated 12 miles (19km) to the west of Edinburgh is **Hopetoun House** ㊴ (www.hopetoun.co.uk; daily Apr–Sept 10.30am–5pm, last entry 4pm), the historic family home of the earls and marquesses of Linlithgow. Begun in 1699 by William Bruce, William Adam completed the building. Most of the original 18th-century furniture and wall coverings can still be seen, as well as opulent gilding and fine classical motifs. The house is set in 150 acres (60 hectares) of parkland. The rooftop offers great views of the Forth bridges.

Linlithgow itself, a few miles further west, is home to the ruins of **Linlithgow Palace** ㊵ (tel: 01506 842 896; daily Apr–Sept 9.30am–5.30pm; Oct–Mar until 4.30pm). Built by James I in 1425, the palace witnessed key events in Scottish history. In 1513 Queen Margaret waited here for the return of her husband James IV unaware of his death at the hands of the English in the Battle of Flodden. In 1542 Mary, Queen of Scots, was born here, and the future Charles I was raised at the palace. Oliver Cromwell wintered at Linlithgow during his 1650 punitive trip to Scotland. A century later the palace was gutted by fire following Bonnie Prince Charlie's retreat from England. The extensive remains give an impressive idea of the scale and splendour of the palace in its heyday.

East Lothian

East of Edinburgh is the benign and affluent terrain of **East Lothian**. Its rolling farmland is ornamented with pretty, coastal villages and the northern coastline is dotted with bays, beaches and bird-haunted islands. The sandy links give it some of the best golf courses in the world.

Visit **Portobello** to savour the faded charm of a delightful, old-fashioned seaside resort. Prosperous Victorian families from Edinburgh spent summers here on the wide sandy beach. Handsome Georgian terraces testify to the town's wealthy past.

Rosslyn Chapel

Southwest of the city lies the former mining village of Roslin and, beyond, the beautiful woodlands of **Roslin Glen Country Park**, which provide the backdrop to **Rosslyn Castle**, constructed by Henry Sinclair, Earl of Orkney, during the 14th century. The Sinclair family are buried in the small **Rosslyn Chapel** ❹ (www.rosslynchapel.org.uk; Mon–Sat 9.30am–5pm, Sun noon–4.45pm), which is elaborately decorated inside with carvings of the Seven Cardinal Virtues and Seven Deadly Sins. Look out for the beautiful **Apprentice Pillar**.

Rosslyn Chapel

The chapel became famous following the huge success of *The Da Vinci Code* by Dan Brown. In the novel it is claimed that the Holy Grail was once hidden at Rosslyn and that the descendants of Jesus and Mary Magdalene can be traced to the chapel.

WHAT TO DO

FESTIVALS

Although Edinburgh has many year-round attractions, the city bursts into life in July and August with a number of separate festivals running concurrently. The city almost comes apart at the seams, with visitors vying for street space with performers, clowns, face painters and numerous small crafts markets. For more information, you can access websites for all the festivals at www.edinburghfestivals.co.uk (for ticket and contact information, see page 132).

Edinburgh International Festival

In the wake of World War II, Edinburgh's Lord Provost, Sir John Falconer, envisaged a great celebration of the arts, which would bring nations closer together and re-establish Edinburgh as a European city of culture on a worldwide stage. In 1947 Edinburgh hosted its first International Festival and, with opera impresario Rudolf Bing at the helm, it was a great success, rapidly becoming one of the foremost festivals of its kind in the world.

Every year, for three weeks in August, all eyes are on the dozens of performances and events in the many theatres of the city centre. Although the first festival was biased towards orchestral music, the modern festival has a comprehensive programme of dance, music, opera and theatre, with some of the finest exponents in every field gracing the stage. The city's ability to stage large-scale performances was considerably enhanced in 1994 with the development of the huge Edinburgh Festival Theatre, which has nearly 2,000 seats and a stage larger than that of London's Royal Opera House. Details

A walk up Arthur's Seat will be rewarded with fantastic views

The Fringe takes over the city every August

of the International Festival programme are available in March each year.

Edinburgh Festival Fringe

The Festival Fringe was born at the same time as the official festival and started as a sometimes irreverent, loose collection of extra performances held in the city. Initially the Fringe consisted of several small theatre companies that were not included in the official festival programme but nevertheless decided to hold performances on the same dates.

Free from the confines of the International Festival's rules and regulations, the Fringe has become synonymous with art that pushes the boundaries, specialising in experimental theatre and stand-up comedy. The Fringe has grown to eclipse its official brother, selling almost 2 million tickets a year. It comprises over 2,800 different shows, with countless performances taking place at all times of the day and night in around 250 venues.

Every year the cream of young artistic and comic talent makes its way to Edinburgh, and the Fringe is arguably the largest showcase for performers in the world. A programme is produced in spring each year covering all the Fringe performances.

ENTERTAINMENT

Theatre and Music

Of course you don't need to visit Edinburgh during the summer festivals in order to see excellent performances of the arts in the city. Companies including the National Theatre of Scotland, the Scottish Opera, Scottish Ballet, the Royal Scottish National Orchestra and the BBC Scottish Symphony Orchestra all mount frequent performances. There are also several major theatres with an ever-changing schedule of touring plays, ballets and musical performances, as well as popular shows featuring international singers and bands.

Although you will find venues scattered throughout the city, the main theatre district is found south of the west end of Princes Street. Off Lothian Road, the **Traverse Theatre** (10 Cambridge Street; tel: 228 1404; www.traverse.co.uk), is Edinburgh's most exciting contemporary theatre, promoting new writing. Also in the vicinity, on Lothian Road, is the elegant concert venue **Usher Hall** (tel: 228 1155; www.usher hall.co.uk), home to the Royal Scottish National Orchestra. Nearby on Grindlay Street is the **Royal Lyceum Theatre** (tel: 248 4848; www.lyceum. org.uk), a refurbished Victorian theatre that stages high-quality classic and contemporary drama. The

What's on?

To find out what's on during your stay pop into a newsagent and buy a copy of *The List* magazine (www.list.co.uk).

glass-fronted **Edinburgh Festival Theatre** on Nicolson Street (tel: 529 6000; www.edtheatres.com) plays an integral role in the International Festival, and is also home to Scottish Opera and Scottish Ballet. West End musicals are staged in the East End **Playhouse Theatre** (18–22 Greenside Place; tel: 0844 871 3014; www.playhousetheatre.com).

Cinemas

Filmgoers are well served in Edinburgh. The refurbished **Cameo** (38 Home Street; tel: 0871 902 5723; www.picture houses.co.uk) was first opened in 1914 and retains an original auditorium, screening art-house and commercial films. Another arty independent is the **Filmhouse** (88 Lothian Road; tel: 228 2688; www.filmhousecinema.com). For block-busters and popcorn there's the 12-screen **Vue** cinema at the Omni Centre (Greenside Place; tel: 08712 240 240; www.my vue.com).

Scottish Nights

A number of companies offer an evening of Scottish dancing along with an 'addressing the haggis' ceremony – traditionally performed on Burns Night. You will find all the paraphernalia of kilts, bagpipes and ceremonial arms along with traditional Scottish food, whisky and dancing. Regular *ceilidh* dances are held at the Assembly Roxy (2 Roxburgh Place; www.edinburghceilidhs.com), which are energetic and lots of fun. There is usually an experienced caller on hand to demonstrate the steps.

Pubs, Clubs and Bars

Edinburgh is a city with an energetic nightlife throughout the year, in part due to liberal licensing laws. Many bars close at midnight or later and clubs at about 3am. The best places to find them are Cowgate and Grassmarket in the

Live music at Tron Kirk

Old Town, and Broughton Street and George Street in the New Town. In the subterranean caverns under Cowgate is popular **Cabaret Voltaire** (36–38 Blair Street), while **City** (1a Market Street) is Edinburgh's own super club. **Cav** (3 West Tollcross) offers the ultimate clubbing experience and **Lulu** (125b George Street) is a club to remember with crystals embedded in the walls. **Opal Lounge** (51a George Street) is a stylish bar appealing to the smart set. Descend the steps to Bramble Bar (16a Queen Street) where cocktails are an art form and rub elbows with the hippest of Edinburgh's drinking set.

For a classic city pub, try the **Guildford Arms**, on West Register Street one block north of the east end of Princes Street. Grassmarket is a lively area for pubs, including the **Last Drop Tavern**, another traditional establishment, with low ceilings and low lighting. Its name is a reference to the gallows that used to stand in the square.

SHOPPING

Edinburgh draws the best of Scottish products to its shops and provides a ready marketplace for goods from the northern Highlands and islands. The major shopping street is Princes Street, where you'll find – among many major British names – Edinburgh's traditional department store, Jenners, a local institution for generations. The store has a wonderful art deco interior to match its ornate exterior. The streets running parallel to Princes Street in the New Town, such as pedestrianised Rose Street and Thistle Street, have smaller shops and boutiques, while the larger upmarket George Street offers a range of designer fashion outlets, as does Multrees Walk (off St Andrew Square). Not to be overlooked, the cobbled Georgian streets in Edinburgh's West End are home to a delightful mix of designer boutiques, organic food stores and other independent retailers.

At the top of the Royal Mile you'll see the typical tourist fare of postcards and tartan, but in the narrow surrounding streets

Tracing Your Ancestors

Edinburgh offers rich opportunities for the ancestor hunter. In New Register House, at the east end of Princes Street (just behind General Register House), there are records of every birth, marriage and death in Scotland since 1855; parish records date from even earlier. For £15 a day you can inspect the records and should be able to trace several generations.

Alternatively, you can try the Scottish Genealogy Society and Family History Centre, where nonmembers may take a research session for £7 a day (Mon–Thu 10.30am–5.30pm, Wed until 7.30pm, Sat 10am–5pm, 15 Victoria Terrace; tel: 220 3677; www.scotsgenealogy.com).

If you don't want to attempt the task yourself, a private company that offers a free initial consultation is Scottish Roots Ancestral Research Service (16 Forth Street; tel: 477 8214; www.scottishroots.com).

there are many individual shops selling antiques, books and collectibles. For alternative fashion and kitsch try Cockburn Street which runs off the High Street section of the Royal Mile.

If it's raining or cold, a couple of undercover shopping options are Princes Mall (which is home to the Tourist Information Centre), on Princes Street next to Waverley Railway Station, and the larger St James Centre (undergoing a major redevelopment

Tartan products are ubiquitous

due for completion in 2020; some shops remain open), on Leith Street at the east end of Princes Street. Ocean Terminal at Leith waterfront also has excellent shopping.

What to Buy

Tartan. This fabric is synonymous with Scotland – the major Scottish families had their own traditional tartan patterns that instantly identified their clan and kinship. If you have any Scottish ancestry, you will be able to find the tartan for you; otherwise, it is a matter of finding a pattern that you like. All new tartan patterns must be registered.

Traditionally tartans are worn in the form of a kilt or traditional Highland dress. The Edinburgh Old Town Weaving Company (on Castlehill) has about 170 tartans for sale but will also custom make a kilt for you.

Woollens. The northern islands produce beautiful, heavy-knitted Fair Isle and Aran sweaters. After the Industrial Revolution cashmere was introduced to the weavers; the garments produced from

Second-hand bookshops abound

this wool make good gifts. Tweed is also produced from wool, and made into jackets, coats and suits.

Books. Edinburgh has long been at the forefront of publishing and printing. It supported the work of the university, which was a major centre of learning from the 16th century, particularly in law, medicine and veterinary practice. A legacy of the publishing industry is the number of bookshops selling second-hand, antiquarian and new books. Blackwell's (formerly James Thin) has the largest bookstore in Scotland (on South Bridge, opposite the university buildings of Chambers Street). The city has a rich association with authors, from Robert Louis Stevenson to Ian Rankin and JK Rowling, and in 2004 it was honoured with Unesco's first City of Literature designation.

Antiques. As a capital city, Edinburgh has its own office for the stamping of gold and silver, with the city's mark found on many antique pieces. If you find an old 'tappit hen' (a traditional drinking tankard), look for the silver assay mark of a castle, indicating an authentic Edinburgh piece.

Jewellery, silver and other crafts. From the days of the Stuart kings, Scottish jewellery was known for the high quality of its workmanship. Use of traditional Scottish materials such as silver – and stones such as carnelian or agate – make for unique pieces. Often local Celtic patterns appear in bracelets, brooches and scarf rings. Traditional craft skills also extend to the manufacture of high-quality pottery and glassware.

SPORTS

Golf. It is traditionally held that Scotland gave golf to the world, and Leith Links is considered the 'home of golf'. Around 10 East Lothian courses participate in the Golf East Lothian Visitor Pass, which offers discount on a 'stay and play' scheme at some of the best golf courses in the area (tel: 01620-892197; www.golfeastlothian.com). It is advisable to book any course in advance.

Just 55 miles (88km) north of Edinburgh is St Andrews, a hallowed destination for golfers from around the world and one of the premier professional courses on the international tour. It is possible to play a round on a day excursion from Edinburgh, although it is difficult to get a starting time on the world-famous Old Course.

There are a number of golf courses in East Lothian

Rugby. Edinburgh is the home of Scottish Rugby Union. West of the city centre is Murrayfield Stadium where Scottish and international games are held throughout the season, including the Calcutta Cup which pits the Scots against their 'auld' enemy the English. For tickets and information, tel: 0844 335 3933.

Athletics. Meadowbank Stadium is the major venue for track and field athletics. It has a schedule of events in summer (tel: 661 5351).

Football

Football is a passion in Scotland. Edinburgh has two teams in the Premier League: Heart of Midlothian (Hearts), playing at Tynecastle Stadium, Gorgie Road (tel: 0871-663 1874; www.heartsfc.co.uk); and Hibernian (Hibs), who play at the Easter Road Stadium (tel: 661 2159; www.hibernianfc.co.uk). Football season runs from August to mid-May.

Hillwalking. Holyrood Park, within the city's boundaries, provides an ideal area for walking, with spectacular views of Edinburgh from Arthur's Seat. The walk up this volcanic peak is steep but within the capability of a normally fit person.

The Pentland Hills, which rise steeply on the southern tip of Edinburgh, provide some delightful hillwalking, the splendid views changing with the seasons.

Skiing. West of the city at Hillend is Midlothian Snow Sports Centre, the longest artificial ski slope in the UK (400 metres/ 1,312ft). Open year round, the centre has all the equipment you need to rent (tel: 445 4433). You will need to have some prior experience of skiing to use the slope; alternatively, lessons are offered.

ACTIVITIES FOR CHILDREN

Edinburgh has plenty of activities for children to enjoy. Take them to **Edinburgh Castle** for stories of heroism and marvellous city views.

At Castlehill nearby, the **Camera Obscura** and **World of Illusions** are popular with children and offer a unique view of the city rooftops. Just be prepared for several flights of stairs to reach the top.

Explore the story of our planet at **Our Dynamic Earth** (www.dynamicearth.co.uk). Here you can witness the Big Bang, experience an earthquake and come face to face with a dinosaur all in one place.

Children will love seeing teddies, dolls, trains and pedal cars up-close at the **Museum of Childhood** and get hands-on with dressing up costumes and games.

Not for the very small or faint hearted, **Edinburgh Dungeon** (www.thedungeons.com) offers a thrilling journey through Scotland's murky past.

Edinburgh Zoo (www.edinburghzoo.org.uk) in Corstorphine has a penguin parade every day at 2.15pm. Over the Forth Road Bridge at North Queensferry, **Deep Sea World** (www.deepseaworld.com) is the site of Scotland's national aquarium. Its underwater tunnel offers a diver's-eye view of the deep.

Every May, the **Imaginate Festival for Children** (www.imaginate.org.uk) holds arts, theatre and dance activities and performances for children aged 8 to 15. The **Scottish Storytelling Centre** (www.tracscotland.org) holds weekly events through the year. During the festival, kids love the street theatre, clowns, face painting and temporary tattooing.

If your children are tired of trudging city streets, take a ride to **Portobello Beach** (on the Firth of Forth), where the long stretch of sand offers a perfect environment for walks, kite flying, or wading and swimming in the sea.

Our Dynamic Earth

Festivals and Events

It is no surprise that Edinburgh has an international reputation for being a festival city. Things reach fever pitch in August when there are no less than six major events, including the International Festival and the Fringe. These, and others throughout the year, are well worth checking out.

Edinburgh International Book Festival: Last three weeks in August. Literary giants from around the world gather for readings, discussions, storytelling and book signings. Includes a much-praised children's programme. Held in Charlotte Square. www.edbookfest. co.uk

Edinburgh International Film Festival: Last two weeks in June. A prominent fixture in the film world featuring premieres, animations, documentaries, cult films and interviews. The main venue is the Filmhouse, with screenings around the city. www.edfilmfest.org.uk

Edinburgh International Jazz and Blues Festival: Late July. The best of national talent and visiting world-class jazz musicians. Various venues. www.edinburghjazzfestival.co.uk

Edinburgh International Science Festival: Three weeks in April. Catering for all levels of knowledge, there are plenty of hands-on experiments, exhibitions, events and lectures. www.sciencefestival.co.uk

Edinburgh Military Tattoo: Three weeks in August. Colourful displays of regimental marching, horsemanship and pipe-and-drum bands performed nightly on the Castle Esplanade. www.edintattoo. co.uk

Hogmanay: Three-day festival of torchlight parades, street theatre and food fairs to usher in the New Year. www.edinburghshogmanay. org

Edinburgh Mela: Two days in late August. World music and dance in a carnival of colour, rhythm and delicious food in Leith. www. edinburgh-mela.co.uk

EATING OUT

The Scots are proud of a cuisine distinct from that of the English, and they have contributed many fine ingredients to the British national palate of cooking styles. The clean air, pure water and acres of open lowlands and hills offer a range of quality produce: from wild game and other meats to fish, seafood, vegetables and fruit. Modern Scottish cooking uses the best of these ingredients, and there are several 'native' restaurants in the city with an international reputation for serving the best in quality and variety.

However, Edinburgh is not just a city of Scottish cuisine. It has restaurants ranging from Indonesian to Thai to Mexican. The city's population of urbane lawyers, academics, doctors and artists demands the best, and the quality of eateries in the city is generally very high. Having established itself as the parliamentary capital of Scotland, Edinburgh attracts interest and investment from the biggest names in the culinary world, ensuring a cutting edge in local cuisine. Accompanying the restaurant scene is a lively café culture, with lots of individual outlets as well as the usual chains.

Traditional Scottish fare

WHEN TO EAT

In restaurants lunch is from noon to 2.30pm, though many pubs serve food all day. Set lunches are a good deal, and many restaurants offer them Monday to Friday. You will also find

numerous sandwich bars and cafés. There are good cafés in Edinburgh Castle, the National Museum of Scotland and the Scottish National Portrait Gallery. High tea is rather more than an afternoon snack; it is generally served between 3pm and 5pm.

Dinner is normally served from 6.30pm to 10.30pm, but many establishments serve later on weekends and during the summer season. Many restaurants, including some of the most renowned, will offer pre- or post-theatre special menus, serving early or late depending on your needs. These are very popular – especially during the festival season – so you should book tables in advance.

WHAT TO EAT

Historically, the Highland farmers and clansmen had meagre diets. The land and the rivers belonged to all-powerful landowners, and taking wild or managed livestock from fields and woods or fish from the rivers was considered poaching. If you were caught, the severe punishments included deportation or even death.

In poorer households, oatmeal formed a major part of the diet, and there were mills in every settlement to grind the meal. Porridge (oatmeal cooked with water and salt) was eaten for breakfast, and oatcakes were served at every meal, supplemented by vegetables and a little protein. Oatmeal is still a popular ingredient used to add fibre and texture. But today's visitors can also sample native meats and seafood in a range of dishes.

> **Taste of Scotland**
>
> *The List's* Eating and Drinking Guide provides listings for Edinburgh and Glasgow; www.list.co.uk. To find details of restaurants that serve traditional Scottish food, visit www.taste-of-scotland.com.

Alfresco eating and drinking in summer – weather permitting

Breakfast

Breakfast can be a feast, even in the smallest B&Bs. It can prepare you for the rest of the day, and it might even see those on a budget through until dinner.

A full Scottish breakfast will always include bacon, sausage, black pudding (blood sausage), eggs, tomatoes, mushrooms and toast. Juice and cereal will also be a part of the full breakfast package. If this is a little too much to eat first thing in the morning, lighter traditional breakfasts include smoked kippers from Loch Fyne or finan haddie (fillet of haddock smoked with peat) poached in milk. Kedgeree is another nutritious option, consisting of a delicious mixture of flaked fish, rice and hard-boiled eggs.

Porridge might sound like a light alternative, but a bowl full of oatmeal is actually very filling. Cool it by pouring milk or cream over it and add salt to taste – or sugar, though the Scots scoff at sweetening it.

Scotland also produces delicious marmalades, jams and honey, particularly from the wild fruits and heather of the northern Highlands.

Soups and Broths

Soups and thick broths have always been popular in Scotland, particularly in winter. Cooks often made a few ingredients go a long way, especially in poorer crofter families in the countryside. The internationally known Scotch broth comprises vegetable soup made with mutton stock and thickened with barley and lentils; cock-a-leekie is a soup of chicken and leeks (authentic only if it contains prunes). You'll also find seafood soups: Cullen skink is a combination of smoked haddock, onions, potatoes and milk; partan bree is cream of crab meat.

Main Dishes

The Scottish countryside offers an abundance of quality fresh ingredients for the table. The woods and moors still have healthy hunting and shooting industries. Partridge, grouse, pheasant and venison all form the basis of very tasty meals. The beef from Aberdeen Angus cattle is considered to be world class and the local lamb is also excellent.

Simple broiled or roasted meat is standard, but you can also find it accompanied by a sauce of some kind (perhaps red wine) or served slow-cooked in a stew with onions and seasonal vegetables.

Haggis is perhaps the most famous Scottish dish. It was originally a dish for the poor, made from parts of the animal left after the major cuts had been taken. Haggis is traditionally made with the 'pluck' of a sheep (the lungs, heart and liver). These parts are boiled for three hours, then the fat is skimmed off and the rest minced. Oatmeal, onion, seasoning, spices and gravy are then added, and the entire mixture is stuffed into a sheep's 'paunch' or stomach (modern haggis may be encased in an artificial skin to avoid bursting). The stuffed skin is then simmered in water for one to two hours.

Always served as hot as possible, the haggis is cut lengthwise and the meat mixture scooped out. The casing is discarded and only the filling is put on the plate. It is traditionally eaten with neeps and tatties (mashed turnip and mashed potatoes).

Delicacies at the Scottish National Gallery of Modern Art café

Fish and seafood are also popular, although catches from the nearby seas and rivers have been diminishing. Salmon was, until recently, a fish available only to rich landowners, caught in private rivers. Smoked sea fish such as haddock or herring were traditionally on a working-class menu, produced in smoking sheds along the coast of the Firth of Forth before being transported the short way to the residential areas of the city.

Today, class lines have been blurred and the most modest of fish dishes have become fashionable. River salmon and trout remain expensive, but the supply has been supplemented in recent years by farmed fish (although aficionados will argue that the taste is not the same as wild fish).

A classic Scottish dish: haggis, neeps and tatties

Smoked salmon can be enjoyed as an appetiser with bread and butter, or the whole fish might be poached as an entrée. You will also find finan haddie or Arbroath smokies (haddock smoked with oak chips).

There are many non-Scottish varieties of fish, but the traditional local method of preparation is to sauté them with a crisp oatmeal coating.

Desserts

The Scots are known for their sweet tooth. Wild fruits from the land – raspberries, blackberries, rhubarb and gooseberries, among others – form the basis of many pies and puddings, often with a crisp coating of oatmeal. Cranachan is a dish of raspberries and cream topped with toasted oatmeal. Atholl Brose is a delicious blend of whisky, honey, cream and oatmeal – a rather adult version of porridge. Auld Alliance, creamed cheese laced with whisky, is traditionally eaten as a spread on toasted bread.

> **Address to a Haggis**
>
> Fair fa' your honest,
>   sonsie face,
> Great chieftain o' the
>   puddin'-race!
> Aboon them a' ye tak
>   your place,
> Painch, tripe, or thairm:
> Weel are ye wordy of a
>   grace
> As lang's my arm.
> – Robert Burns (1786)

Cheese can also be found in great variety, served with oatcakes. Try Dunlop, not unlike cheddar; Lanark Blue, a Roquefort-style blue cheese; or Bonchester, a Camembert-style offering.

Shortbread was originally an oatmeal bread served at Christmas, though it was a food carried over from pagan times. Made in a circle and pinched around the edge with the finger, it was meant to symbolise the rays of the sun that would bring rebirth to the land in spring. The oatmeal was subsequently replaced by finer milled flour to create today's shortbread biscuit, which is rich in sugar and butter.

WHAT TO DRINK

Whisky

Without doubt, the king of Scottish drinks is whisky, a concoction that the Scots are said to have invented. (The Irish might dispute that!) *Whisky* is a Gaelic word derived from the phrase *uisge beatha*, meaning 'water of life'. It is a blend of pure spring water, malted barley or grain and yeast, which is distilled and then aged in oak barrels. But this simple recipe belies the richness and variety of the finished product.

Two factors are important for the flavour of the finished product. The first is the water from which the whisky is made, imparting the particular taste of each brand. Scottish water is considered particularly good for the production of a distilled alcohol, but it tastes different in different parts of the country (some waters are filtered through peat, imparting a particular flavour to the finished drink). The second factor is the shape of the still used in the distillation process. Each shape produces a different finished alcohol, the clear spirit that is then aged in oak casks.

The nearest working distillery to the city, Glenkinchie, produces a very soft lowland malt, which is a perfect introduction to single malts for the beginner. Distillery tours are available. You will find that most bars and hotels will have a range of malts and blended whiskies for you to try. The shop in the Scotch Whisky Experience has a very extensive range – including many rare and unusual examples – from all parts

High Tea

The prim ladies for whom Edinburgh is famed – in the style of Miss Jean Brodie – would shop in town and take tea at one of the fine hotels or cafés as a finale to their afternoon. This tradition continues, a perfect activity for visitors to sit and relax in a genteel environment after a day of sightseeing (between 3pm and 5pm). In addition to the sandwiches and cream cakes, you may be tempted by a potato scone, or a slice of Dundee cake (a rich fruitcake decorated with almonds), or a black bun (a cake flavoured with dried fruit ginger mixed with cinnamon and brandy). Jams and honey made with produce from the countryside are a delicious accompaniment.

of Scotland, and staff can give you information about the particular attributes of each drink (see page 39).

Single Malts

Whiskies produced from malted barley and bottled direct from the barrel are called 'single malts' and each of the several hundred produced by different distilleries in Scotland is distinctive in its taste. Lowland malts (from the area in the south of Scotland) are softer in style and flavour; Speyside malts (from farther north, east of Inverness) are considered the 'cream' of single malt; Highland and island malts (Islay, Arran, Jura, Skye, Mull)

There are over 700 pubs in Edinburgh

are unique in their flavour, sometimes heavy with heather peat, producing a 'medicinal' taste.

Malt whisky is aged for a number of years in oak barrels before being bottled; the minimum time is three years, but some are aged for 15 or 20. Aging refines the taste and imparts the distinctive colour to the whisky.

Blended Whisky

In the past both the quality and quantity of whisky production would vary, and the flavour of many single malts was not suited to the taste of the mass population. In the 18th century, a group of distillers decided to create a standard product that could be produced in batches for consistency and palatability. They began to produce whisky from grains other than malted barley and to mix different whiskies (malts and non-malts) together, producing the blended whiskies of today. Blends contain whiskies of different ages – up to 40 different whiskies in one blend. When a blend has an age on the label, it is the age of the youngest whisky in the blend.

The art of whisky blenders is a fine one. They smell different aged whiskies to create a blend, very much as a perfumer creates a fragrance. Only a few individuals have the 'nose' for the job, and this has often been a hereditary occupation, passed down from father to son.

Drambuie
Drambuie was said to be Bonnie Prince Charlie's favourite drink. He bequeathed its secret recipe to his friend MacKinnon

Enjoying a glass of whisky at the Scotch Whisky Experience

of Straithard in gratitude for organising the prince's escape from the English army in 1746. The drink was made in small quantities for family consumption until 1909, when it went on general sale. The MacKinnon family still owns the company and has continued to keep the recipe a secret while making a success of the commercial production. Interestingly, the recipe has been passed down through the female line of the family.

> ### Whisky business
>
> Whisky is generally served neat, with ice, or with a little water. If you drink it with soda water, you might get a friendly lecture from a Scotsman.

Glavya

First produced in 1940, *glavya* (meaning 'very good') blends whisky, herbal oils, honey and sugar. Ronald Morrison and George Petrie, a chemist, worked together at their Leith blending works to perfect the taste. To preserve its secrecy, the recipe is known by only three people at any one time.

Beer

Edinburgh's former prosperous brewing industry lives on in the Caledonian Brewery (www.caledonianbeer.com), and the distinctive smell of warm hops often blows across the city on the prevailing breeze. The Caley, as the brewery is affectionately known, dates back to 1869 and today produces various types of beer that are on sale in pubs throughout the city. It has won many accolades for its brews in recent years and concentrates on traditional methods of production.

Its most famed beer is 80/- ('Eighty Shilling') named after the cost of the excise duty on a consignment in times past. Stronger beer had more excise duty, weaker beer less. Other Caledonian beers include Deuchars IPA, Flying Scotsman and Old Contemptible.

PLACES TO EAT

We have used the following symbols to give an idea of the price for a three-course meal (without drinks), per person, including VAT:

££££ over £45	**££** £22–32
£££ £32–45	**£** below £22

ACROSS EDINBURGH

Howies ££ *Two locations: 10–14 Victoria Street (tel: 225 1721) and 29 Waterloo Place (tel: 556 5766), www.howies.uk.com.* Howies Victoria Street is a small rustic place in the medieval Old Town, while Howies Waterloo Place boasts Georgian elegance at the foot of Calton Hill. Expect French and Scottish cuisine with lots of game and fish, and menus that change daily. Open daily for lunch and dinner.

Stac Polly £££ *Two locations: 29–33 Dublin Street (tel: 556 2231) and 38 St Mary Street, (tel: 557 5754), www.stacpolly.com.* Stac Polly has gained a reputation throughout the city for exciting Scottish dishes using local ingredients, for which it's won a number of awards. The traditional settings such as the labyrinth of cellars at Dublin Street add to a real Scottish evening. Dublin Street Brasserie (££) upstairs opens for lunch Monday–Saturday; main restaurant for dinner daily. St Mary's opens for lunch Monday–Friday and for dinner Monday–Saturday. All have vegetarian options.

OLD TOWN

Amber Restaurant ££ *The Scotch Whisky Experience, 354 Castlehill, Royal Mile; tel: 477 8477, www.amber-restaurant.co.uk.* Lunch here is informal and good value, with delicious soups and sandwiches alongside heartier mains. For dinner, first-rate service is accompanied by an innovative menu including Scottish estate-bred beef and lamb, prime game, North Sea monkfish and the freshest vegetables. Open daily for lunch and dinner.

Angels with Bagpipes £££ *343 High Street, tel: 220 1111, www.* angelswithbagpipes.co.uk. Contemporary style meets Old Town at this delightful restaurant close to St Giles Cathedral. Head chef Fraser Smith creates original menus based on Scotland's finest food larder. Open daily for lunch and dinner.

Castle Terrace ££££ *33–35 Castle Street, tel: 229 1222, www.* castleterracerestaurant.com. This Michelin-starred dining experience by Edinburgh Castle exudes culinary confidence. Edinburgh-born chef Dominic Jack presents modern British cuisine influenced by innovative French techniques, using only the finest Scottish ingredients. Brown tones with a hint of purple are the basis for a very stylish dining room. Open Tuesday–Saturday for lunch and dinner.

David Bann's Vegetarian Restaurant £ *56–58 St Mary's Street, tel: 556 5888,* www.davidbann.co.uk. A popular restaurant serving an excellent range of vegetarian dishes throughout the day to a mixed clientele, from Edinburgh students and locals to visitors. Open daily for lunch and dinner.

Dubh Prais £££ *123b High Street, Royal Mile, tel: 557 5732, www.* dubhpraisrestaurant.com. This small, cellar restaurant serves the best in Scottish cuisine. Venison and salmon dishes appear regularly on the menu. Open Tuesday–Saturday for dinner only.

Field ££ *41 West Nicholson Street, tel: 667 7010,* www.fieldrestaurant. co.uk. Having worked in Michelin-starred restaurants the chefs here know what's what. You'll find good honest cooking such as parsnip and apple soup to start followed by home-smoked trout and fig tartin, complemented by a world-class wine list. Open Tuesday–Saturday for lunch and dinner.

Hanam's £ *3 Johnston Terrace, tel: 225 1329,* www.hanams.com. For something different try this restaurant with Middle-Eastern and Kurdish cooking. Shish kebabs – Iranian or Kurdish style – chargrills and vegetarian options feature on the menu. No alcohol but you can bring your own. Open daily for lunch and dinner.

Namaste Kathmandu ££ *17/19 Forrest Road, tel: 220 2273, www.* namastektm.co.uk. Authentic, delicious Indian and Nepalese cuisine can be found a few yards away from the National Museum. Many unusual, tasty dishes served in a dark, incense-laden atmosphere. Open daily for lunch and dinner.

Ondine £££ *2 George Bridge, tel: 226 1888, www.ondinerestaurant.* co.uk. This gorgeous seafood restaurant is set in an elegant dining room with panoramic views over Old Town. Carefully selected sustainable produce is paramount. Set menus are available for lunch and pre-theatre. Open Monday–Saturday for lunch and dinner.

Pancho Villas Restaurant ££ *240 Canongate, Royal Mile, tel:* 557 4416, www.panchovillas.co.uk. Owner Mayra Nuñez ensures a great Latin atmosphere in this informal Mexican restaurant, which is a great place to chill out after a day's sightseeing. Open Monday–Saturday for lunch and dinner, Sunday dinner only.

Tower Restaurant ££££ *At the Museum of Scotland, 18–27 Chambers Street, tel: 225 3003, www.tower-restaurant.com.* With a sleek modern interior and great views, the Tower presents a Scottish menu with 'nouvelle' twist, including exquisite shellfish and Argyll oysters. Open daily for lunch and dinner.

Wedgewood the Restaurant £££ *267 Canongate, tel: 558* 8737, www.wedgewoodtherestaurant.co.uk. Using the best local ingredients, this Royal Mile establishment creates fabulous Scottish dishes bursting with flavour, such as roast monkfish with oyster fritter, and mustard-crusted lamb loin. Open daily for lunch and dinner.

The Witchery by the Castle ££££ *352 Castlehill, Royal Mile,* tel: 225 5613, www.thewitchery.com. Set just below the castle Esplanade, the two historic dining rooms are striking in their splendour and are lit only by candles at night. Scottish and European fare on offer, with fresh seafood a speciality. Good value pre- and post-theatre suppers are available. Open daily for lunch and dinner.

NEW TOWN

Contini Risorante ££ *103 George Street, tel: 225 1550*, www.contini.com. Northern Italian flavours abound in this classy, tiled former bank turned bistro-bar slap bang in the city centre. Formerly known as the Centotre, it is still run by the same family and continues to serve delicious food, as well as coffees and cocktails. Open daily for breakfast, lunch and dinner.

Dusit ££ *49a Thistle Street, tel: 220 6846*, www.dusit.co.uk. Delivering some of the most consistently good food and service in Edinburgh, Dusit sets the standard for Thai cuisine with its contemporary, perfectly executed dishes. Open daily for lunch and dinner.

L'Escargot Bleu ££ *56 Broughton Street, tel: 557 1600*, www.lescargotbleu.co.uk. This engaging restaurant is very French, from the red-chequered tablecloths and posters on the wall to the friendly staff. But with one exception: they use the very best Scottish produce. Open Monday–Saturday for lunch and dinner, (open Sundays during the Festival in August).

Gusto ££ *135 George Street, tel: 225 2555*, www.gustorestaurants.uk.com. A Modern, open-kitchen Italian restaurant with stainless-steel decor and bustling atmosphere: a typical trattoria with a modern twist. The modern feel compliments traditional Italian dishes from minestrone, bruschetta, pizza, pasta and grilled meats to tiramisu and ice cream. Open daily for lunch and dinner.

Henderson's of Edinburgh £ *94 Hanover Street, tel: 225 2131*, www.hendersonsofedinburgh.co.uk. Edinburgh's original vegetarian/whole-food restaurant is still as popular as ever, with its lively cosmopolitan atmosphere, plus live jazz and other music genres in the evening. Organic wines. Open daily for lunch and dinner.

The Honours £££ *58a North Castle Street, tel: 220 2513*, www.thehonours.co.uk. Local chef Martin Wishart has been a star in the city since 1999 with his Michelin-starred restaurant in Leith. His establishment in New Town boasts a brasserie-style French menu using Scottish ingredients to a high standard. Open Tuesday–Saturday for lunch and dinner.

Magnum Bar & Restaurant ££ *1 Albany Street, tel: 557 4366,* www.themagnum.webeden.co.uk. Large bar with comfortable stylish seating areas. The chefs here use fresh, local ingredients to create Scottish dishes such as Cullen skink and cranachan, alongside game, beef and seafood plates. Open daily for lunch and dinner.

Number One ££££ *1 Princes Street (at the Balmoral Hotel), tel:* *557 6727,* www.restaurantnumberone.com. This Michelin-starred restaurant oozes style and panache without being pompous. Culinary treats include scallops with sweetcorn purée, chorizo and pine nuts, and Borders' roe deer, rainbow chard, sausage, hazelnuts and pistachio. They are all complemented by a fine wine list. Open daily for dinner only.

Pickles £ *56a Broughton Street, tel: 557 5005,* www.getpickled. co.uk. Located beneath L'Escargot Bleu (see page 111), this quirky little place is ideal for a light bite and a drink. Delicious platters featuring Scottish cheeses or meat come with, naturally, a huge range of pickles and sides. Open daily 4.30pm–late.

The Pompadour by Galvin ££££ *Caledonian Hotel, Princes Street, tel: 222 8975,* www.thepompadourbygalvin.com. Brothers Chris and Jeff Galvin have brought their culinary genius to possibly Edinburgh's most elegant and formal dining room. You'll find modern classy French cuisine created using the best of Scottish ingredients. Open Wednesday–Saturday for dinner only.

The Stockbridge Restaurant £££ *54 St Stephen Street, tel:* *226 6766,* www.thestockbridgerestaurant.co.uk. For that special dinner this delightful, intimate restaurant certainly hits the spot. Owner and head chef Jason Gallagher brings flair to the first-class seasonal produce. Open Tuesday–Sunday for dinner only.

Valvona and Crolla ££ *19 Elm Row, tel: 556 6066*, www.valvona crolla.co.uk. A most wonderful Italian restaurant, at the rear of a fabled deli. Open daily for breakfast and lunch only (Sunday opens at 10.30am, rest of the week 8.30am). A second branch (11 Multrees Walk, tel: 557 0088), with the Vincaffè on the ground floor and the Ristorante on the first floor, are both open for dinner too.

Wildfire £££ *192 Rose Street, tel: 225 3636*, www.wildfire restaurant.co.uk. Chargrilled Aberdeen Angus steaks are a highlight here, along with the changing seafood menu featuring dishes such as baked Cajun salmon fillet and Provençal seafood stew. Open daily for lunch and dinner; closed Monday lunch.

LEITH

Fishers in Leith ££ *1 Shore, Leith, tel: 554 5666*, www.fishers bistros.co.uk. A compact, homely seafood restaurant looking out over the Water of Leith. Try the delicious Isle of Barra scallops or tuck into the Aberdeen smoked haddock fillet. Open daily for lunch and dinner.

The Kitchin ££££ *78 Commercial Quay, Leith, tel: 555 1755*, www. thekitchin.com. This top-end Michelin starred restaurant, headed up by Tom Kitchin, operates the philosophy 'From Nature to Plate.' Maybe start with hand-dived Orkney scallops, follow with loin of roe deer and finish with Perthshire plum and ginger soufflé. Open Tuesday–Saturday for lunch and dinner.

Roseleaf £ *23/24 Sandport Place, Leith, tel: 476 5268*, www.rose leaf.co.uk. Quirky family run bar-café with a lively atmosphere and great home-cooked food, from turkey pie to beetroot burger. Wide range of drinks and, unusually, cocktails served in teapots. Open daily 10am–1am.

The Shore Bar and Restaurant ££ *3 Shore, Leith, tel: 553 5080*, www.fishersbistros.co.uk. This historic hostelry prides itself on its Scottish seafood. For a cheaper option try the Shore bar classics. Regular live jazz and folk music. Open daily for lunch and dinner.

A–Z TRAVEL TIPS

A Summary of Practical Information

A

ACCOMMODATION (see also Camping, Youth Hostels and the list of Recommended Hotels starting on page 135)

Edinburgh offers an extensive range of accommodation: luxury and boutique hotels, historic houses, more modest hotels, boarding houses, simple bed-and-breakfast establishments, backpackers' hostels and campus accommodation. Should you wish to stay for a substantial period of time, there are also self-catering options usually available on a weekly basis, as well as more expensive serviced apartments. VisitScotland produces brochures listing a range of accommodation in Edinburgh and the Lothians, which you can request by calling their information line, tel: 0845 859 1006. You can also book accommodation on this line or through www.visitscotland.com.

Hotels and guesthouses that have been independently inspected and approved by VisitScotland (the Scottish Tourist Board) are given ratings according to the quality of the accommodation. Star gradings range from one star (fair and acceptable) to five stars (exceptional/world class).

In the high season (July–September), and especially in August during the month of the Edinburgh Festivals, the city becomes particularly crowded and rooms are at a premium. Hogmanay (December and early January) is another busy time. Should you intend to visit during these periods, you are strongly advised to book accommodation as far in advance as possible.

However, if you do find yourself in Edinburgh without a hotel reservation, head for one of the city's Tourist Information and Accommodation Centres (on Princes Street or at Edinburgh International Airport), where the staff will try to find a room for you.

In publicity materials, prices for rooms are usually quoted for a double room per night. Breakfast is usually included, but do check before making a reservation. Rooms in most hotels have en suite bathrooms, but some B&Bs (particularly at the budget end of the market) may have shared facilities. Always make sure you know what is included in the price of the room. VAT is always included in the price, but service charges (between 10 percent and 15 percent) might not be. Many hotels, however, do not add this charge.

For those on a budget who do not want to stay in a backpackers' hostel, all three Edinburgh universities offer accommodation in their halls of residence over holiday times. This is cheaper than most hotels but not always cheaper than a B&B in a private house. Edinburgh First, at the University of Edinburgh, is the most central (tel: 651 2007, www.edinburghfirst.co.uk), offering en suite double rooms from around £45–70 per person, some with views of Arthur's Seat. There's also Napier University (tel: 455 3713, www.napier. ac.uk) and Edinburgh Conference Centre (Heriot Watt University, tel: 451 3669, www.edinburgh-conference.com).

AIRPORTS (see also Getting There)

Edinburgh International Airport (tel: 0844 448 8833, www. edinburghairport.com) lies 7 miles (11km) west of the city. In addition to receiving flights from airports throughout Britain, nonstop flights land here from many European cities. British Airways and Virgin Atlantic both run comprehensive services to and from London Heathrow. EasyJet operates low-cost flights from London Gatwick, Luton and Stansted, while Aer Lingus and Ryanair fly from Dublin. United Airlines fly non-stop from Newark and Chicago in the US. Airlink bus 100 connects the airport with the city (Waverley Station) every 10 minutes during the day at a cost of £4 one way, £7 return. A tram also runs from the airport to the city (York Place), at a cost of £5 one way, £8 return. Taxi fare is approximately £20–25, with travel time around 30 minutes, and they are available from just outside the arrivals hall.

Glasgow International Airport (tel: 0844 481 5555, www. glasgowairport.com) is just over an hour's drive from Edinburgh. It receives non-stop flights from North America (daily flights from Newark, Philadelphia and Toronto). Frequent buses link the airport to the city centre (£6.50 one way, £9 return). Trains to Edinburgh from Queen Street Station run every 15 minutes during the day (otherwise every half hour), taking 50 minutes (approx £12.50 one way off peak). Frequent buses run to Edinburgh from Buchanan Street bus station taking about 70 minutes (approximately £7.30 one way, £11 return).

For bus and rail travel information in Scotland contact Traveline (tel: 0871 200 2233, www.travelinescotland.com).

B

BICYCLE HIRE

Edinburgh takes care of its cyclists, offering cycle paths and allowing cyclists to use separate bus lanes in the city centre. Cyclists can also take advantage of the Old Town's narrow alleyways, where cars cannot travel. Because the centre of Edinburgh has many hills and inclines, cycling here requires a certain level of fitness.

A map of cycle routes is available from the tourist information centres at the airport and Princes Street. Bikes can be rented from Le Tour Edinburgh (http://letour-edinburgh.com, tel: 07415 640 296). See also www.visitscotland.com/cycling.

BUDGETING FOR YOUR TRIP

Britain is a relatively expensive place to visit. Here are a few guidelines to help with budget-planning:

Accommodation: £125–175 for a double room including breakfast per night in a medium hotel.

Meals: Dinner £24–30 per person in a moderate restaurant with wine.

Domestic airfare: From £90 (roundtrip/return) from London Heathrow to Edinburgh.

Car hire: £240 per week (£48 per day) for a medium-sized vehicle, including VAT and unlimited mileage, but not insurance.

Bus and tram travel: £1.50 single trip; £3.50 for a day pass.

Family passes: Check with VisitScotland (www.visitscotland.com)

for any offers on travel or attraction entrance charges.

Museums and galleries: Approximately £6.50–14 for an adult; many city museums and galleries are free.

Theatre tickets: £24–40 for a mid-price ticket.

Bus tour of the city: £14.

C

CAR HIRE

If you plan to spend most of your time in Edinburgh's compact city centre a vehicle will probably be more of a hindrance than a help, as parking is difficult. However, if you plan to take trips into the surrounding countryside, you will want to hire a car.

All major car-hire companies have desks at Edinburgh's airport (**Arnold Clark**, tel: 0131 278 3100, www.arnoldclarkrental.com; **Avis**, tel: 0844 544 6004, www.avis.co.uk; **Europcar**, tel: 0871 384 9900, www.europcar.co.uk; **Hertz**, tel: 0843 309 3025, www.hertz.co.uk; **National**, tel: 0871 384 3453, www.nationalcar.co.uk), and it is possible to pick up a car immediately upon your arrival in the city. If you are visiting from outside the UK it can be cheaper to reserve your car from home rather than when you arrive.

Many companies have a minimum age (usually 21) for drivers, and you will need to have your full licence (with at least a year's driving experience) when you pick up the car. Credit cards are the preferred method of payment. Insurance covers collision damage and theft, but you may have to pay an excess.

CLIMATE

Southern Scotland has a temperate climate influenced by its proximity to the Atlantic Ocean, though Edinburgh in particular is affected by the North Sea. The summers are warm and wet; the winters are cold and wet. Even in summer, cold spells can occur and the weather can change quickly.

Average monthly temperatures are as follows:

	J	F	M	A	M	J	J	A	S	O	N	D
°C	4	5	7	10	14	17	19	18	15	11	7	6
°F	39	41	44	50	58	62	66	64	59	52	44	43

CLOTHING

With Edinburgh's often chilly climate, a trip requires several different types of clothing even if you travel in summer. A rainproof outer layer is a must whatever time of year you travel, along with an umbrella. In winter, a thick coat or jacket, gloves and a hat will keep you warm in cold spells, when the wind can bite.

On warm summer days, T-shirts, light shirts and trousers or light dresses make ideal clothing. But always carry an extra layer just in case, and take a light sweater or jacket for the evenings. Comfortable shoes are a must for the daytime.

CRIME AND SAFETY (see also Emergencies)

The centre of Edinburgh is fairly safe compared to other large European cities. All the same, you should take the usual precautions against theft. Any theft or loss must be reported immediately to the police in order to comply with your travel insurance. If your passport is lost or stolen, you should also inform your consulate.

City streets are relatively busy. This makes walking safe, but always make sure that you walk in well-lit streets late at night.

CUSTOMS AND ENTRY REQUIREMENTS

Entry requirements. Citizens of most EU countries don't require a visa (just a passport) to visit Scotland.

Citizens of Australia, Canada, New Zealand, South Africa and the US need only a valid passport to enter the UK for tourist visits of up to six months. All passports must be valid for six months beyond the intended length of stay in the UK.

Upon arrival you will have to complete an entry card stating the address where you will be staying. The immigration officer will stamp your passport, allowing you to stay in Britain for a specific length of time. If your plans are uncertain, ask for several months so you don't have to apply for an extension later. Provided you look respectable and have sufficient funds to cover your stay, there should not be a problem.

Your best starting point for a visa-related enquiry concerning entry to the UK is to contact the UK Foreign and Commonwealth Offices visa website (www.ukvisas.gov.uk).

Currency. There are no currency restrictions when entering or leaving the UK, for either British or foreign currencies.

D

DRIVING (see also Car Hire)

If you are bringing your own car or one from Europe, you will need the registration papers and insurance coverage. The usual formula is the Green Card, an extension to existing insurance that validates it for other countries. Don't forget your driver's licence.

Rules and regulations. Remember to drive on the left. Pay special attention at crossings and roundabouts. Traffic that is already in the roundabout has the right of way over cars waiting to enter the roundabout, and the rule is to give way to the right.

Drivers and passengers must use seat belts. Motorcycle riders must wear a crash helmet, and a driver's licence is required for all types of motorcycle. The minimum age for mopeds is 16, and 17 for motorcycles and scooters.

In built-up areas the speed limit, unless indicated to the contrary, is 30mph (48kmh); on motorways 70mph (112kmh) and on other inter-city roads 60mph (96kmh) except when these are dual carriageways when it is 70mph (112kmh). The prevailing speed limit is posted on road signs at the side of the road.

Edinburgh has a number of special lanes for buses and taxis only. These usually operate 7.30–9.30am and 4–6.30pm, easing the traffic flow at peak times. One-way streets also help to prevent bottlenecks. If you plan to drive around the city, invest in a good map.

Road conditions. There are three main types of roads: motorways (expressways), A roads (trunk roads that link all the major towns) and B roads (rural roads). Driving conditions in the UK are generally very good, and all A roads are of good quality.

Fuel costs. Petrol is expensive in the UK: approximately £1.07–£1.17 per litre. Most garages have self-service pumps, all of which give measurements in litres. You will find stations in all major towns. The normal hours of operation are 7am–10pm, but this can vary enormously. Some petrol stations are open 24 hours a day.

Parking. You can park at the side of the street provided there are no restrictions. Many streets will have areas for resident parking with fines for those who break the rules. Street parking is expensive, with costs of £1.60–£3.20 per hour. Both street parking and car parks throughout the city operate a 'Pay and Display' system – you purchase a ticket from a machine and display the ticket on your dashboard.

Assistance. Most hire cars come with coverage from a reputable recovery or breakdown service. The Automobile Association (AA), the Royal Automobile Club (RAC) and Green Flag are well known.

Road signs. Britain has the same basic system of pictographs in use throughout Europe. The *Highway Code* is the official booklet of road usage and signs, available at most bookshops.

E

ELECTRICITY

The standard electrical supply in the UK is 240 volts AC, 50 Hz. All visitors (except South Africans) will need an adapter (with square

3-pin plugs) for any appliance brought from home, as well as a converter unless the appliance is equipped with one. Adapters are available at airport shops. Most hotels have special sockets for shavers and hairdryers that operate on 240 or 110 volts.

EMBASSIES, CONSULATES AND HIGH COMMISSIONS

Many countries have consuls or other representatives in Edinburgh, but others have representation only in London.

Australia: Australian High Commission, Australia House, Strand, London WC2B 4LA, tel: 020 7420 3690.

Canada: Canadian Consulate, tel: 07702 359916, email: canada.consul.edi@gmail.com.

Ireland: Consulate General of Ireland, 16 Randolph Crescent, Edinburgh EH3 7TT, tel: 226 7711.

New Zealand: New Zealand Consulate, 5 Rutland Square, Edinburgh EH1 2AX, tel: 222 8109.

South Africa: South African High Commission, South Africa House, Trafalgar Square, London WC2N 5DP, tel: 020 7451 7299.

US: American Consulate General, 3 Regent Terrace, Edinburgh EH7 5BW, tel: 556 8315.

EMERGENCIES (see also Health and Medical Care and Police)

The emergency telephone number throughout the UK is **999**.

G

GAY AND LESBIAN TRAVELLERS

There are several gay pubs and clubs in the city centre. There is a monthly magazine called *Scotsgay*, which also has a website www.scotsgay.co.uk. *The List*, which is the club, theatre and cinema guide for Edinburgh and Glasgow, also has a gay section. Support is offered by the LGBT Helpline Scotland (www.lgbt-helpline-scotland.org.uk), open Tue–Wed noon–9pm.

GETTING THERE (see also Airports)

By rail. From central London and the London airports there are rail links (through King's Cross Station) to Edinburgh's Waverley Station run by East Coast Railway (www.eastcoast.co.uk). The journey takes about 4.5–5 hours. Contact National Rail Enquiries (within the UK tel: 08457 484950, www.nationalrail.co.uk), www.scotrail. co.uk or www.raileurope.com for details of this and other British and European train travel.

By bus. National Express offers a comprehensive network of coach/ bus services throughout the UK, with regular service from London's Victoria Station to Edinburgh. You can connect as well via other cities and towns as part of an itinerary. Further details and timetables are available by phone in the UK only (tel: 08717 818 181, www.national express.com). For local bus (and rail) travel information in Scotland contact Traveline (tel: 0871 200 2233, www.travelinescotland.com).

By car. Edinburgh is in the north of the UK, reached from England either directly via the A1 (in the east) or via the M6 (in the west); the M6 connects with the M74 and then the A702 to reach Edinburgh. The driving time is approximately 7 hours on either route, depending on traffic and weather conditions.

From Ireland the Irish Sea Ferry crosses Dun Laoghaire (pronounced 'Dun Leary') to Holyhead, Wales; from there, take the M6 for the onward drive to Edinburgh. Ferry services from Northern Ireland operate from Larne to Troon and Belfast to Stranraer.

GUIDES AND TOURS

There are several types of tours in the Edinburgh region. Themed walking tours are a great favourite. Options include:

Auld Reekie Tours (tel: 557 4700, www.auldreekietours.com). Various macabre tours, including the Terror Tour (10–11.30pm), the Ghost and Torture Tour (6pm and 8pm) and a tour of haunted underground vaults (noon, 2pm, 4pm and 5pm). Starts at Tron Kirk.

Mercat Tours (tel: 225 5445, www.mercattours.com). Various daytime historical walks and haunting evening walks through the Old Town's narrow alleyways. Starts at the Mercat Cross outside St Giles.

The Real Mary King's Close see page 44.

The Edinburgh Literary Pub Tour (tel: 0800 169 7410, www. edinburghliterarypubtour.co.uk). Tours through the Old Town with commentary by costumed actors depicting literary characters. Begins at 7.30pm at the Beehive Inn in the Grassmarket. Runs May–Sept daily; Jan–Mar Fri, Sun; Apr and Oct Thu–Sun; Nov–Dec Fri only.

Rebus Tours (tel: 553 7473, www.rebustours.com). Readings and locations from Ian Rankin's bestselling crime novels. Starts noon and 3pm at the Royal Oak pub, Infirmary Street. Pre-booking necessary.

Sandemans Tour (www.newedinburghtours.com). Free city tour every day at 11am and 1pm. Meet at Starbucks on the Royal Mile; you can book on line or just turn up. Also has specialist paid-for tours.

Bus tours. There are also bus and coach tours to attractions in the city, the surrounding Lothians area and even further north into Scotland. Pick-up points for these are along Waverley Street outside the railway station. Bus tours to outlying areas such as Lowlands, Highlands and St Andrews are also available. One company operating a range of options is Rabbie's Trail Burners (meeting point: Rabbie's Café, 6 Waterloo Place; tel: 226 3133, www.rabbies.com). Trips start from £31.

H

HEALTH AND MEDICAL CARE

No vaccinations are needed for a visit to the UK. Tap water is safe to drink. The National Health Service offers free emergency treatment or first aid to all visitors. Free treatment does not apply to dentistry or to consulting an optician. However, for treatment of a more complicated nature or a pre-existing condition, charges will be made. Citizens of European Union countries are entitled to medical treatment under reciprocal arrangements and should bring their European Health Insurance Card (EHIC). It is always sensible to take out comprehensive medical insurance for your trip.

The main 24-hour Accident and Emergency hospital is Edinburgh Royal Infirmary which is in Little France off the Old Dalkeith Road (tel: 536 1000). A 'pay as you go' service provided by experienced doctors can be found at 40 Colinton Road (tel: 0845 1196 049, www.gpplus.com).

A range of 'over-the-counter' drugs are available for everyday ailments. A qualified pharmacist (chemist) will offer advice about the medication you need. There is a dispensing pharmacy open until 7pm at Boots the Chemist (101–3 Princes Street, tel: 225 8331), opening till 8pm on Thursday.

For emergency dental problems, there is a walk-in centre at 3 Chalmers Street (Mon–Fri 9am–3pm). It is advisable to arrive in the morning, (tel: 536 4800, which also gives advice for out-of-hours emergencies).

HOLIDAYS

The following dates are public holidays in the city (generally known as 'bank holidays' in the UK). This means that offices and banks will be closed, but shops and restaurants remain open. When a bank holiday falls on a Saturday or Sunday, the following Monday will be taken as the official holiday:

Scottish national holidays
New Year, 1–2 January
Good Friday
Easter Monday
May Day, first Monday in May
Spring Holiday, last Monday in May
Christmas Day and Boxing Day, 25–26 December
Additional local holidays in Edinburgh
Edinburgh Spring Holiday, third Monday in April
Victoria Day, third Monday in May
Edinburgh Autumn Holiday, third Monday in Sept

L

LANGUAGE

Many place names throughout Scotland are derived from Gaelic names, and words and phrases from the old Scots dialect (called 'Lallans') are still in common use.

LOST PROPERTY

The lost-property department at Waverley Station is on platform 2 (tel: 550 2333). Note that lost property (including that which is left in taxis) found in and around the city centre may be handed in to the police headquarters at Fettes Avenue (tel: 311 3131).

M

MAPS

A selection of Edinburgh maps can be found in tourist information centres. These will be adequate for sightseeing, particularly on foot. If you intend to travel by car, a more detailed map will be needed. The A–Z Map Company produces detailed maps of all cities in the UK; these can be bought at major newsagents, bookshops and large petrol stations. Another good map to take with you is the Insight Fleximap Edinburgh, laminated for durability and easy folding.

Scottish/Gaelic English
auld lang syne days long ago
aye yes
bairn child
ben mountain
bide a wee wait a bit
biggin building
bonny/bonnie pretty

brae hillside
brig bridge
burn stream
cairn pile of stones
ceilidh song and story gathering
clachan hamlet
croft small land-holding
dinna fash yersel' don't get upset
dram measure of whisky
firth estuary
glen valley
haud yer wheesht shut up
inver mouth of river
ken know
knock knoll
kyle strait
lassie girl
links seaside golfcourse
linn waterfall
loch lake
mull promontory
skirl sound of bagpipes
strath river valley
thunderplump thunderstorm
wynd lane

MEDIA

The main Scottish newspapers are the *Herald* and the *Scotsman*. Major British daily broadsheet newspapers available around the nation include the *Times*, the *Telegraph*, the *Guardian* and the *Independent* which all cover world events. Daily tabloid newspapers include the *Sun* and the *Daily Mirror*. A number of newsagents in the city centre sell foreign newspapers, including American titles (US papers might be one or two days old).

Five terrestrial television networks operate in Britain: BBC1, BBC2, ITV, Channel 4 and Five, plus numerous digital channels. BBC Scotland produces topical regional programming. Some hotels will provide satellite services such as Sky and CNN. The BBC provides national and local radio services. BBC Radio Scotland can be found on FM 92.4–94.7 and MW 810kHz/370m.

A particularly useful entertainment magazine is *The List*, published every two weeks and covering music, theatre, cinema, arts and sports in both Edinburgh and Glasgow (www.list.co.uk).

MONEY

The official currency of Britain is the pound sterling (£); the pound is divided into 100 pence.

Three Scottish banks issue their own notes, which are not, technically, legal tender in England and Wales, although many shops will accept them and English banks will readily change them for you.

Notes are printed in denominations of £5, £10, £20, £50 and £100. Coins are found in denominations of 1p, 2p, 5p, 10p, 20p, 50p, £1 and £2.

Banks and building societies are open Monday–Friday for foreign exchange. There are foreign exchange offices in the Marks and Spencer department store (54 Princes Street) and at the American Express office (69 George Street), as well as at Waverley Station and at Edinburgh Airport.

Most banks and building societies will have ATMs that accept international debit cards. Most machines will also dispense cash advances on major credit cards. City centre branches of most banks can be found in and around George Street.

Traveller's cheques can be cashed at banks, bureaux de change and many hotels, although the best rates are normally available at banks.

Credit cards are widely accepted for payment in hotels, restaurants and shops, although not always in small guesthouses and B&Bs.

O

OPENING HOURS

Banks are generally open Monday–Friday from about 9am until 4.45 or 5pm. Offices are open Monday–Friday 9am–5pm. Post offices open Monday–Friday 9am–5.30pm and Saturday 9am–12.30pm (until 5.30pm for major post offices).

Shops are usually open Monday–Saturday 9am–5.30pm (extended opening until 8pm on Thursday) and Sunday 11am–5pm. Hours may be extended during summer.

Restaurants typically open daily noon–2pm and 6–10.30pm, but these hours will differ with the seasons and especially during the Festival. Some restaurants close on Sunday or Monday and some do not open for lunch; others are open all day. Normal opening hours for pubs are Monday to Thursday 11am–midnight, Friday and Saturday until 1am. Normal Sunday hours are 12.30pm–11pm, but extensions until 1am are not uncommon. As in the rest of the UK, smoking is banned in pubs, bars and restaurants.

P

POLICE (see also Crime and Safety and Emergencies)

British police have a worldwide reputation for friendliness and the ability to give courteous directions. Police uniforms are black and you will see foot patrols (unarmed) operating regular routes in the city. For all emergencies dial **999**.

POST OFFICES

Post offices can be recognised by red signs with yellow lettering. The Central Post Office in Edinburgh is in the Princes Mall Shopping Centre, Waverley Bridge (tel: 524 6901). It offers mailing services, currency exchange and cash transfer, and it sells items such as stamps, postcards and phone cards. Many postcard shops and newsagents will also sell stamps. In outlying areas, smaller post offices also act as small stores but will not have currency exchange or cash transfer services.

Postage: within the UK, 62p; to Europe and the rest of the world, airmail 97p.

PUBLIC TRANSPORT (see also Airports)

Buses and trams. Edinburgh has a bus system that travels to all parts of the city as well as out to the coast and the surrounding countryside. The routes are split between several private companies, the main ones being Lothian Buses (tel: 555 6363, www.lothianbuses.com) and First in South East and Central Scotland (www.firstgroup.com/ukbus/scotland_east). The fare for adults is £1.50, and 70p for children, for any distance. You can pay per trip on the bus (Lothian Buses require exact change) or buy a day ticket (£3.50 per adult; £2 per child), although the ticket is not transferable between Lothian and First Bus services run from early morning until late into the evening, with several night buses operating on main routes into and out of the city. The main bus station is on St Andrew Square.

Edinburgh Trams (tel: 555 6363, www.edinburghtrams.com) work in partnership with Lothian Buses. Trams run for 15 stops between York Place in New Town and Edinburgh Airport. Tickets must be bought from vending machines, located at each stop, before entering the tram. Ticket prices for the city zone are the same as for Lothian buses (see above) and day tickets can be used on both buses and trams. Tickets can also be purchased online or via the Transport for Edinburgh mobile app.

All public transport timetables are available on telephoning 0871 200 2233. Here you can also get details of transport options for people with special needs.

City tour buses run from 9.35am until dusk every 20 minutes in summer (every 30 minutes in winter) on a route that takes in most of the city's major attractions. A day ticket costs £14; you can hop on and off the buses for a single daily fare as you visit the sights. Tickets for city bus tours and other bus and coach services can be purchased at the Edinburgh Information Centre, 3 Princes Street.

Taxis. Black taxis (like those in London) run all around the city. You can hail them on the street or pick them up at ranks (at Waverley Station and at the west end of East Street). City firms include: City Cabs: 228 1211; Central Taxis: 229 2468; Comcab: 272 8000.

Trains. Edinburgh's Waverley Station is a major rail hub, providing service to all parts of the UK. Numerous local services are ideal for those who wish to visit other Scottish towns such as North Berwick, Dunbar, Linlithgow, Stirling, St Andrews, Perth and Glasgow.

T

TELEPHONE

The country code for the United Kingdom is **44**. When dialling from outside the UK, the city code for Edinburgh is **131**; if you are phoning Edinburgh from within the UK, dial **0131**.

Phone calls can be made from call boxes and kiosks using coins, credit cards and calling cards. Some older boxes might accept coins only. Phonecards of various denominations can be purchased from newsagents, post offices and tourist information offices.

To call the Operator for UK calls, tel: 100, for international calls, tel: 155. Directory enquiries are provided by several companies. Numbers include 118 500, 118 365, 118 212 and 118 118.

Mobile (cell) phone coverage is not as good in Scotland as the rest of the UK, with rural areas particularly neglected by some service providers. Edinburgh, however, has good coverage, including 4G. You will need a GSM cellular phone. If visiting from abroad, the cheapest option is to buy a local UK SIM card to use in the GSM phone – incoming calls will be free and local calls inexpensive.

TICKETS

Tickets for the Edinburgh International Festival are available from festival offices at The Hub, Castlehill, EH1 2NE (general enquiries tel: 473 2099, box office tel: 473 2000, www.eif.co.uk).

For Fringe performances contact the Fringe box office, which can be found at 180 High Street (a little below St Giles Cathedral), Edinburgh EH1 1QS (tel: 226 0026, www.edfringe.com).

Military Tattoo tickets can be purchased from the Military Tattoo office at 32 Market Street, Edinburgh EH1 1QB (tel: 225 1188, www.edintattoo.co.uk). Telephone, postal and web bookings can be made from early December of the preceding year; early booking is strongly advised.

There is no official central booking agency for theatre performances at other times of the year; tickets can be purchased directly from individual venues (see page 87).

TIME ZONES

The UK runs on Greenwich Mean Time (GMT) in winter and on British Summer Time (BST) in summer. The clocks are put forward one hour on the last Saturday in March, and put back again on the last Saturday in October. The following chart shows the times in various cities during the summer.

San Francisco	New York	**Edinburgh**	Sydney	Auckland
4am	7am	**noon**	9pm	11pm

TIPPING

Hotels and restaurants often add a service charge (10 percent to 15 percent) to the bill, in which case there is no need to tip. If service has not been satisfactory, this charge may be deducted from the bill. If the charge has not been added to the bill, 10 percent is an average tip for satisfactory service.

Taxi drivers and hairdressers do not include service charges; a tip of 10 percent is normal for satisfactory service.

TOILETS

There are public facilities in department stores along Princes Street, at the west end of Princes Street Gardens, Castlehill and Waverley Station (also with showers). There might be a small charge for the use of some facilities. Most tourist attractions will also have public toilet facilities.

TOURIST INFORMATION

The Edinburgh Information Centre, 3 Princes Street, tel: 0845 22 55 121 www.edinburgh.org, is open seven days a week year round. There is also a branch at Edinburgh airport.

If you require additional information about Edinburgh and Scotland you can also contact VisitScotland (Ocean Point One, 94 Ocean Drive, Edinburgh EH6 6JH, tel: 524 2121, www.visitscotland.com). If you plan to take in other areas in the UK, VisitBritain (www.visitbritain.com) has information on things to do, accommodation, transport and more.

W

WEBSITES AND INTERNET ACCESS

Here are a few sites to help you plan your trip on the internet. Others can be found in the contact details for individual attractions, hotels and restaurants in this pocket guide.

Edinburgh

www.edinburgh.org Edinburgh and the Lothians tourist office
www.edinburghfestivalcity.com Edinburgh's summer festivals
www.list.co.uk The List events magazine online
www.edinburghshogmanay.com New-year celebrations
www.ewht.org.uk World Heritage City
www.edinburghguide.com Edinburgh Guide – news, events, info

www.thisisedinburgh.com Comprehensive website all about the city, including some hidden gems

Scotland

www.visitscotland.com VisitScotland

www.visitbritain.com VisitBritain

www.scotsman.com *The Scotsman*

www.undiscoveredscotland.co.uk Undiscovered Scotland

www.historic-scotland.gov.uk Historic Scotland

www.nts.org.uk National Trust for Scotland

www.eventscotland.org Forthcoming festivals and sports events

Edinburgh is well serviced when it comes to internet access and has several cafés that offer free Wi-fi, such as Brew Lab, Caffè Nero, Freemans and BeanScene. Increasingly, hotels and guesthouses offer internet and wireless access, and B&Bs are beginning to follow suit. The airport has computers available for passenger use to access the internet and Wi-fi hotspots.

Y

YOUTH HOSTELS (see also Accommodation)

The Scottish Youth Hostels Association central booking office is at 7 Glebe Crescent, Stirling, FK8 2JA (tel: 01786 891 400, central reservations: 0845 2937 7373, www.syha.org.uk). You can make reservations directly through the website.

The flagship SYHA Edinburgh Central (9 Haddington Place, tel: 0131 524 2090) has dormitory rooms that start from £14, doubles from £32.95 per person. Edinburgh Metro hostel is only open in summer, but has a great location off Cowgate and over 300 single rooms (11/2 Robertson's Close, tel: 556 8718).

A non-affiliated youth hostel that lives up to its name is the Smart City Hostel, situated very centrally, just off the Royal Mile (50 Blackfriars Street, tel: 524 1989, www.smartcityhostels.com). Dormitory rooms start from £10, doubles from £39 per person.

Recommended Hotels

Edinburgh offers accommodation ranging from five-star hotels to guesthouses, B&B establishments and rooms in private homes (see page 115). They are typically priced per double room per night, and include breakfast in the room charge. There might be a single person supplement if only one person uses the room. Hotels will also quote a rate for dinner, bed and breakfast.

Guesthouses often have rooms that are just as luxurious as hotel rooms, though not always with en suite bathroom facilities. Run by local families, they often offer value for money, traditional Scottish cuisine and a warm welcome.

High season in Edinburgh is from June to mid-September (with an extra-high season during the Edinburgh International Festival and Fringe Festival), when it is important to book if you want to guarantee a certain type of room.

The price categories below are average daily rates per double room with two people sharing, including breakfast and VAT.

££££	over £250
£££	£175–£250
££	£100–£175
£	under £100

OLD TOWN

Edinburgh City Hotel ££ *79 Lauriston Place EH3 9HZ, tel: 622 7979, www.edinburghcityhotel.com.* Housed in a neo-Gothic mansion dating back to *c.*1879, this hotel offers good value accommodation just 10 minutes from the Royal Mile. The menu at Simpsons restaurant features local produce. 52 rooms.

G&V Royal Mile Hotel ££££ *1 George IV Bridge EH1 1AD, tel: 220 6666, www.quorvuscollection.com.* Perfectly placed on Edinburgh's Royal Mile, this splendid luxurious boutique hotel certainly has the wow factor. Fabulous bold design and stunning use of colourful textiles. 136 rooms.

Ibis Edinburgh Centre South Bridge ££ *77 South Bridge EH1 1HN, tel: 292 0000,* www.ibis.com/edinburgh. Rising from the ashes of the Cowgate fire, this is not just another chain hotel. The decor is impeccable and the rooms have extremely comfortable beds. 259 rooms.

Inn on the Mile ££ *82 High Street EH1 1LL, tel: 556 9940,* www.the innonthemile.co.uk. Beautiful building in the old part of the city just down the road from castle. Stunning bedrooms with original features and lots of nice touches – including complementary tea cakes. 9 rooms.

Jurys Inn Edinburgh ££ *43 Jeffrey Street EH1 1DH, tel: 200 3300,* www.jurysinns.com. A large, modern hotel with comfortable, spacious rooms. Excellent location near Waverley Station. coffee bar and separate restaurant. 186 rooms.

Radisson BLU Hotel, Edinburgh £££ *80 High Street, Royal Mile EH1 1TH, tel: 557 9797,* www.radissonblu.com. On the Royal Mile, this hotel has everything on its doorstep. With its exterior the tall facade of a traditional Edinburgh tenement, the luxury rooms inside are modern. Facilities include leisure club, swimming pool and free Wi-fi. 238 rooms.

The Scotsman £££ *20 North Bridge EH1 1TR, tel: 556 5565,* www. thescotsmanhotel.co.uk. A luxury boutique hotel produced from a successful make-over of *The Scotsman* newspaper offices. Comfortable rooms have all mod cons, and there's a health club with pool. 68 rooms.

NEW TOWN

Ballantine West End Hotel £ *6 Grosvenor Crescent EH12 5EP, tel: 225 7033,* www.ballantraewestend.co.uk. Family-run hotel in an elegant row of Victorian terrace houses overlooking gardens. 11 rooms.

The Balmoral ££££ *1 Princes Street EH2 2EQ, tel: 556 2414,* www. roccofortehotels.com. A Princes Street landmark, overlooking the

Georgian streets right at the heart of the shopping district yet only a couple of minutes from the Royal Mile. This luxury hotel has high levels of service, and features an indoor pool, sauna, special spa packages, fitness centre and two restaurants. A two-minute walk from the railway station (rooms are soundproofed). 188 rooms.

The Bonham ££ *35 Drumsheugh Gardens EH3 7RN, tel: 274 7400,* www.townhousecompany.com/thebonham. Only five minutes from the west end of Princes Street, this Victorian house has been transformed into a boutique hotel with contemporary designer interiors. Highly respected restaurant. 49 rooms.

Frederick House Hotel £ *42 Frederick Street EH2 1EX, tel: 226 1999,* www.frederickhousehotel.com. This hotel has been converted from a listed chamber office building and offers comfortable accommodation in the central New Town. Free Wi-fi. 44 rooms.

The George Hotel ££ *19–21 George Street EH2 2PB, tel: 225 1251,* www.thegeorgehoteledinburgh.co.uk. This large hotel is situated on one of the main streets of the New Town. Its listed Georgian facade houses a luxury interior with a grand, marble foyer. Restaurant. Limited parking. 249 rooms.

The Glasshouse Hotel £££ *2 Greenside Place EH1 3AA, tel: 525 8200,* www.theglasshousehotel.co.uk. Situated near the east end of Princes Street, this is a state-of-the-art building hidden behind the facade of an old church. Some rooms surround a 2-acre roof garden. The exterior rooms have splendid views to the New Town or across the Firth of Forth. Evening meals can be taken in the cosy Snug with roaring log fire and direct access to the roof terrace. 77 rooms.

Howard Hotel £££ *34 Great King Street EH3 6QH, tel: 557 3500,* www.thehoward.com. The Howard – three Georgian townhouses dating from 1829 – is a luxurious and intimate hotel offering the best in hospitality. Individually designed rooms with sumptuous appointments and decor. Butler service, restaurant and small car park. 18 rooms.

Motel One Edinburgh-Princes £ *10–15 Princes Street EH2 2AN, tel: 550 9220,* www.motel-one.com/en/hotels/edinburgh. Behind the historic facade lies stylish budget accommodation in a great central location. The One Lounge bar and café in the lobby also serves breakfast. 140 rooms.

Roxburghe Hotel £££ *38 Charlotte Square EH2 4HQ, tel: 240 5500,* www.theroxburghe.com. Designed by architect Robert Adam and situated on Edinburgh's grandest square. Swimming pool, fitness club, sauna and solarium. 198 rooms.

Crown Plaza – Royal Terrace Hotel ££–£££ *18 Royal Terrace EH7 5AQ, tel: 557 3222,* www.primahotels.co.uk/royal. Part of a Georgian terrace on the northern flank of Calton Hill, with a superb view of the Firth of Forth. Rooms with sumptuous contemporary decor and unique glass bathrooms, pool and large private garden. 97 rooms.

Tigerlily £££ *125 George Street EH2 4JN, tel: 225 5005,* www.tigerlilyedinburgh.co.uk. This boutique hotel, in a converted Georgian townhouse, beautifully decorated rooms and suites, including the glamorous Georgian Suite. Restaurant and cocktail bar. 33 rooms.

Waldorf Astoria ££££ *Princes Street EH1 2AB, tel: 222 8888,* www.waldorfastoriaedinburgh.com. Formerly The Caledonian, and the Grand Dame of the city for many years, this hotel offers a range of rooms and suites, many of which have a view of the castle. Full fitness complex. 241 rooms.

DEAN VILLAGE

Channings ££ *12–16 South Learmonth Gardens EH4 1EZ, tel: 315 2226,* www.channings.co.uk. Five Edwardian townhouses have been transformed into a hotel retaining its original features but with comfortable, individually styled rooms. A 10-minute walk from Princes Street. Bar/brasserie and a sun-deck garden at the rear. 42 rooms.

TOLLCROSS

Best Western Bruntsfield Hotel ££ *69–74 Bruntsfield Place EH10 4HH, tel: 229 1393, www.thebruntsfield.co.uk.* Overlooking the parkland of Bruntsfield Links, 1 mile (2km) from the city centre, with shops and restaurants within strolling distance and a major bus route to town outside the door. Restaurant and bar. 67 rooms.

MURRAYFIELD

Edinburgh Lodge ££ *3 West Coates EH12 5JD, tel: 337 3682, www.edinburghlodge.co.uk.* This elegant Victorian house – now a small, family-run hotel – is on the road from the city to the zoo, just a 15-minute stroll to Edinburgh's centre. Bar, parking. 12 rooms.

SOUTHSIDE

Classic Guest House £ *50 Mayfield Road EH9 2NH, tel: 667 5847, www.classicguesthouse.co.uk.* Formerly an elegant Victorian house, situated near bus route to city (a five-minute journey into town) or 20 minutes on foot. Good value for money. 7 rooms.

Lauderville Guest House £ *52 Mayfield Road EH9 2NH, tel: 667 7788, www.laudervilleguesthouse.com.* A registered Victorian terrace house located 4 miles (6km) south of the city, close to main bus routes. Family run, with tastefully decorated rooms, some with four-poster beds, and free Wi-fi. Excursions can be arranged. Lounge and gardens, parking. 10 rooms.

LEITH

Holiday Inn Express Edinburgh – Waterfront £ *Britannia View, Ocean Drive, Leith EH6 6JJ, tel: 555 4422, www.expressedinburgh. co.uk.* A modern hotel in the heart of Leith overlooking the Royal Yacht *Britannia*. Offers modern, comfortable rooms at budget-conscious prices. 102 rooms.

Malmaison £££ *1 Tower Place, Leith EH6 7BZ, tel: 468 5000*, www.malmaison.com/locations/edinburgh. Award-winning with lavish decor, the beautifully styled rooms make this one of the best mid-range hotels in the UK. Brasserie with well-stocked bar, 24-hour fitness room. 100 rooms.

INVERLEITH

Inverleith Hotel ££ *5 Inverleith Terrace EH3 5NS, tel: 556 2745*, www.inverleithhotel.co.uk. Family-run Georgian house hotel overlooking the Royal Botanic Garden. Excellent full Scottish breakfast; 10 rooms of varying sizes with en suite facilities.

CITY OUTSKIRTS

Dalhousie Castle & Spa £££ *Bonnyrigg, Midlothian EH19 3JB, tel: (01875) 820153*, www.dalhousiecastlehotelandspa.com. This 13th-century castle, set in lovely grounds, boasts a dungeon restaurant and a spa with a Roman-style sauna. Some rooms feature arched ceilings and huge picture windows. Other rooms are located in a nearby lodge (specify Castle Rooms when booking if that is your preference). Seven miles (11km) from Edinburgh city centre. 35 rooms.

Dalmahoy Marriott Hotel & Country Club £££ *Long Dalmahoy, Kirknewton EH27 8EB, tel: 333 1845*, www.marriott.com. A grand mansion, 6 miles (10km) to the west of the city and 3 miles (5km) from the airport, set in 1,000 acres (400 hectares) of wooded parkland. Leisure facilities include two championship golf courses, swimming pool, sauna, solarium and gym. 215 rooms.

INDEX

Berlitz pocket guide
Edinburgh
Eleventh Edition 2015

Written by Lindsay Bennett
Updated by Jackie Staddon and Hilary Weston
Edited by Rachel Lawrence
Cartography updated by Carte
Picture Editor: Tom Smyth
Production: Rebeka Davies and Aga Bylica

Photography credits: Alex Knights 38, 54; Bill Wassman/Apa Publications 22, 23; David Cruickshanks/Apa Publications 5TC; Douglas Macgilvray/Apa Publications 4MR, 19, 26, 30, 32, 33, 53, 56, 83, 84, 93, 97, 105; Getty Images 8; iStock 15, 37; Mockford & Bonetti/Apa Publications 1, 2TL, 2TC, 2MC, 2ML, 3TC, 3M, 3M, 3M, 3M, 4ML, 4ML, 4TL, 4TL, 4/5M, 5MC, 4/5T, 6TL, 6ML, 6ML, 7B, 7T, 20, 25, 28, 34, 39, 40, 42, 43, 45, 46, 47, 49, 50, 57, 59, 60, 63, 64, 65, 66, 68, 69, 71, 73, 75, 76, 77, 78, 81, 89, 92, 95, 99, 101, 106; Pete Bennett/Apa Publications 17; Photoshot 51

Cover picture: 4Corners Images

Every effort has been made to provide accurate information in this publication, but changes are inevitable. The publisher cannot be responsible for any resulting loss, inconvenience or injury.

Contact us

At Berlitz we strive to keep our guides as accurate and up to date as possible, but if you find anything that has changed, or if you have any suggestions on ways to improve this guide, then we would be delighted to hear from you.

Berlitz Publishing, PO Box 7910, London SE1 1WE, England.
email: berlitz@apaguide.co.uk
www.insightguides.com/berlitz

phrase book & dictionary
phrase book & CD

Available in: Arabic, Brazilian Portuguese*, Burmese*, Cantonese Chinese, Croatian, Czech*, Danish*, Dutch, English, Filipino, Finnish*, French, German, Greek, Hebrew*, Hindi*, Hungarian*, Indonesian, Italian, Japanese, Korean, Latin American Spanish, Malay, Mandarin Chinese, Mexican Spanish, Norwegian, Polish, Portuguese, Romanian*, Russian, Spanish, Swedish, Thai, Turkish, Vietnamese
*Book only